A Yucatan Kitchen

Regional Recipes from Mexico's Mundo Maya

By Loretta Scott Miller

PELICAN PUBLISHING COMPANY

Gretna 2003

To Adelida Kantun, who taught me an appreciation of her culture along with many of the recipes in this book, and to the countless Mayan cooks who have preserved a great culinary legacy through centuries of creativity and devotion

It is impossible to imagine this book without the help and support of my husband, Ken, and the generosity of our dear friends Joanna and Jorge Rosado, who contributed family recipes, cultural insights, and encouragement every step of the way.

The word "Pelican" and the depiction of a pelican are trademarks of Pelican Publishing Company, Inc., and are registered in the U.S. Patent and Trademark Office.

Printed in the United States of America

Published by Pelican Publishing Company, Inc.
1000 Burmaster Street, Gretna, Louisiana 70053

Table of Contents

FOREWORD

The regional cuisine of Mexico's Yucatan peninsula is a unique blend of Mayan, Mediterranean and Caribbean flavors. Instead of the chile-based sauces found in mainland Mexico, the Yucatan depends on aromatic spice blends called *recados*, which it uses to flavor its soups, stews and roasts.

In recent years, North American chefs have begun to discovered the versatility of recados, and are using them in their own versions of tropical Mayan and Yucatecan dishes.

The body of recipes handed down by the Maya are what clearly sets the cuisine apart from mainland Mexican cooking. Bite into a crispy *Panucho* or glide your fork into a chaya-wrapped brazo and you will experience a culinary connection with a 3,000-year-old culture that has endured foreign conquest, civil war, industrial and technological revolutions, not to mention fast-food invasions.

From its complex tamales wrapped in banana leaves, to its pit-roasted meats basted with aromatic spice blends, it is a cuisine as rich in history as it is in flavor.

One might be tempted to divide the cuisine into two categories: Mayan-influenced dishes, and Spanish or Mediterranean- influenced dishes from the post-conquest era. But that would oversimplify the case and leave out important contributions from the thousands of Lebanese immigrants who have added to the culinary mix, as well as borrowings from North America and France during the last two centuries.

Mainland Mexicans consider the Yucatan an exotic destination, not only for its Mayan culture, but also for its remote location, at the southeastern tip of Mexico. The region includes three Mexican states of Campeche, Yucatan and Quintana Roo, where the Caribbean resorts of Cancun, Cozumel and Playa del Carmen are located.

Like a big thumb, the peninsula juts up into the Gulf of Mexico, pointing north to New Orleans, which is 600 miles away. Cuba is 125 miles from the

FOREWORD continued

peninsula's northeastern edge in the State of Quintana Roo. A ferry now transports visitors and their cars from Tampa, Florida, across the Gulf to the Port of Progreso, Yucatan, in 36 hours.

Despite the advent of modern transportation, the region's history is one of geographic isolation. Cut off from central Mexico by jungle and swampland, until the 1950s when the first road was built, the Yucatan had little contact with Mexico City and turned to the sea for commerce. Its first trading partners were Cubans and Caribbean Islanders. After the conquest, Yucatecans traded directly with North Americans and Europeans, unimpeded by regulation from Mexico City.

At one point in its history, the region broke off from newly independent Mexico and toyed with the idea of allegiance to the United States. But when it was faced with its own civil war, known as the Caste Wars, in mid-19th century, it turned to Mexico City for help and eventually reunited with Mexican and became part of its federation of states.

In the late 19th and early 20th centuries, the Yucatan became home to thousands of Christian Lebanese seeking refuge from the Ottoman empire and Islam. Along with their Catholic religion, they brought culinary traditions, which have been incorporated into the region's cuisine in a unique and delicious "fusion" of flavors and textures, combining, for example, Lebanese kibbehs with Yucatecan pickled red onions.

At the turn of the last century, the Yucatan achieved great wealth through the cultivation and sale of henequen or sisal, a plant that is processed into fiber for rope and twine. Worldwide demand for this product made millionaires of many in the region. The wealthy owners of henequen haciendas not only did business abroad, particularly in the American mid-West, they also sent their sons to France to study, and took their wives to New Orleans to shop.

>>>>>

FOREWORD continued

Henequen brought more than money to the region. As foreign business ties strengthened, foreign social exchanges increased and eventually led to marriages that have had a lasting influence on the Yucatan's culture and especially its cuisine. The Spanish colonial imprint may be strongest, but French and North American flavors, ingredients and techniques are also evident. It is not unusual, for example, to come across recipes in old regional cookbooks for "Chocolate Fudge Cake" and "Hot Fudge", obvious imports from the American heartland.

Some of the recipes in this book were adapted from these old regional cookbooks, others came from the private collections of friends, from haciendas and restaurants, but most were taught to me by Adelida Kantun, a woman of Mayan ancestry who began cooking professionally at age 18.

Although Adelida can barely read or write, she keeps an immense storehouse of culinary knowledge and knowhow in her head, and has a deep respect, bordering on reverence, for fresh ingredients. Along with recipes, techniques, and cultural insights, she also taught me that good cooking requires caring and patience.

Neither the first nor last word on Yucatecan cooking, this is a personal collection that I am sharing in the hope of inspiring others to go into the kitchen and experiment with good, fresh ingredients and a sense of adventure. If you do, you will not only be rewarded with a delicious meal, but you will also be enriched with insight into the rich and complex culture and cuisine of the Yucatan.

Buen Provecho

Yucatan Pantry

Many of the ingredients used in the Yucatan — black beans, bay leaves, capers, cilantro, cumin, cinnamon, clove, garlic, mint, olives, oregano — will be familiar to all but the neophyte cook. Here is a list of special ingredients, utensils and cooking techniques you will want to know about:

Achiote — also called Recado Rojo and Recado Colorado because of its brick red color — is the best known recado or seasoning blend in the Yucatan. The hallmark of Yucatecan cooking, Achiote is made from annatto seeds, garlic, cumin, oregano, onion, salt, pepper, and sometimes allspice, cinnamon and clove, depending on the brand. (See Resource Directory for sources outside Mexico.)

Banana leaves, *hojas de platano*, are used to wrap tamales, fish, chicken and other foods for baking, grilling, steaming or stewing. Outside Mexico, look for them in Asian or Hispanic markets, where they are usually sold frozen. Once thawed, the leaves are ready for use. If you have access to fresh banana leaves, pass them over a flame to soften them before using.

Cebellina looks like chives, but with slightly wider leaves. You can substitute green onion tops or chives.

Chaya, a leafy green vegetable unique to the Yucatan and parts of Central America, is a powerhouse when it comes to protein, vitamins and minerals. Spinach and Swiss chard are good substitutes. (See Resources)

Chile See Habanero and Xcatic

Cilantro, a leafy green herb used in salads, salsas, soups and as a garnish.

Condimento Espanol, used in many rice dishes, is little more than a yellow coloring, with traces of salt and dextrose. In Cuba, Puerto Rico and other Caribbean islands it is called Bijol. Imitation saffron is a good substitute. It really doesn't impart any flavor.

>>>>>

Pantry continued

Escabeche is a recado or seasoning mixture made of black peppercorns, cinnamon, Mexican oregano, cloves, bay leaves, and cumin. Prepared escabeche mixtures are available in the Yucatan, but it is easy to make your own blend, as you would likely have these ingredients on hand anyway.

Habanero chiles come in an array of colors ranging from deep green to golden yellow and red orange. Little fireballs, the indigenous habaneros are roasted and mashed with salt and vinegar or sour orange juice into salsas, and added whole into a simmering pot of beans, broth or tomato sauce for added zip. When used this way, be sure the chile doesn't break open and spill its fiery seeds and veins into your dish.

Lard, rendered pork fat, admittedly has a bad name in the U.S. and Canada. For people with restricted diets, lard should be avoided. The rest of us should remember that lard has less cholesterol than butter and great staying power in tamales, not to mention its wonderful flavor. But if you can't get pure, fresh lard, you might as well substitute oil.

Lima, not to be confused with limon, the commonly used Mexican lime, is an especially sweet, aromatic variety of lime used to make the Yucatan's famous Sopa de Lima. It is distinguished by the navel-like bump on its blossom end. Best substitute is a Myers lemon or similar mild, aromatic lemon.

Masa means dough but refers primarily to the ground corn mixture (not corn meal) used to make tortillas, tamales and atole. Buy fresh masa where you buy tortillas. It can also be made from "masa harina" or flour for tortillas. Four cups of this flour is equal to about 1 kilo (2.2 lbs.) of dough.

Oil most used is vegetable or corn, but for seafood, always use olive oil.

Oregano grown in the Yucatan is preferred. You can substitute Mexican oregano, but not Mediterranean oregano because it will not have the same flavor.

Pantry continued

Plantains or platano macho are sliced and sauteed, mashed and fried, quartered and boiled. This typically Caribbean ingredient is a requisite garnish for Huevos Motulenos and Arroz Con Pollo.

Recado Negro or Chilmole is made with chiles blackened over a fire, thus making this recado difficult to duplicate. Other ingredients include allspice, cumin, black pepper, garlic and oregano

Sour orange or *naranja agria* is unique to the region. Seville oranges can be substituted or use a 50-50 blend of mild vinegar and fresh sweet orange juice. Never use frozen or canned juice if you expect to approximate the true flavors of the Yucatan. If you can't get fresh oranges, use lemons, limes or substitute watered-down or very mild vinegar. One sour orange, depending on its size, yields about ½ cup of juice.

Vinegar is used in many recipes in place of sour orange juice. However, the vinegar in the Yucatan is very mild, only 2 percent acid, and fruity tasting. Consider a watered-down cider vinegar or some other mild vinegar such as rice vinegar as an approximation. Don't ever use full strength cider vinegar in these recipes.

Xcatic is a long, slender chile that ranges in color from pale greenish-yellow to deep yellow-orange. Like the habanero, it is used whole in most dishes. It doesn't have near the heat of the habanero, but it can be quite hot, like a lot of chiles. Milder alternatives are the guero or yellow banana pepper.

Utensils

Blenders are commonly used to make sauces and other dishes in the Yucatan, and throughout Mexico.

Comal, a flat cast aluminum, iron or tin disc is used for charring or roasting vegetables and making tortillas. Although handy, it is not essential. You can use a cast-iron griddle or skillet to roast and char vegetables. If you are going to make tortillas, you should invest in a comal.

Food Processor can successfully be used in place of a blender and I find it essential for making such dishes as Frijol Colado, Ha' Si-Kil Pac and Torta de Cielo.

Mortar and pestle or molcajete is useful for mashing chiles or grinding herbs and spices.

Spice or coffee grinder is especially good for grinding dry spices such as peppercorns and allspice.

Steamer to cook chaya, tamales and other wrapped foods such as Ninos Envueltos. You can always improvise a steamer by putting a plate upside down in the bottom of a stock pot or Dutch oven, and placing your food on top. The idea is to keep the food out of the water.

NOTE: All oven temperatures given in this book are Fahrenheit.

Techniques

Roasting or charring vegetables is one of the most important techniques in mastering flavorful Yucatecan dishes. The best utensil for this process is a comal, a flat metal disk of cast aluminum or cast iron, that can withstand high heat. (You can also roast chiles and garlic cloves right next to the flame on a gas stove.) When roasting, keep turning the vegetable to attain even blackening all over. Yes, you want to blacken or "char" the food. In some cases, you peel off most of the outer blackened skin. The easiest way to peel roasted tomatoes or chiles is to steam them in a tightly closed plastic or paper bag for about 10 minutes. Peel or rub off the charred skin under running water.

Seeding Roma or plum tomatoes is easiest if you slice them lengthwise and remove the seeds with your finger, a small spoon or blunt knife. To seed a hot chile, use rubber gloves, slice lengthwise and cut out the white veins as well as the seeds. Habanero and xcatic chiles are generally not seeded. Both are used whole; habaneros are also mashed along with their seeds for salsa.

Toasting is a technique used to freshen dried herbs and spices as well as seeds and nuts. Use a heavy-bottomed dry skillet, comal or griddle for stove-top toasting on low to moderate heat and watch carefully to prevent burning. If you have a large quantity and prefer to use the oven, spread ingredients on a dry baking sheet and toast at 325 degrees until they begin to brown.

Tenderizing octopus can be tricky. A few days in the freezer helps to break down the tissue, thus tenderizing it; others swear by a good pounding with a wooden mallet, and finally, the addition of vinegar while boiling should help.

Recados and Salsas

Like the curries of India and the moles of Oaxaca, recados are aromatic blends of herbs and spices. Used as rubs, marinades and sauce bases, recados come in a paste or brick form, in dry mixes and as a liquid. These flavorful mixes, with their ancient Mayan roots, are the basis for complex marinades and rubs used by the most creative chefs exploring Latin cuisine in the United States today.

The most commonly used recados are Achiote (also called Recado Rojo because of its brick-red color), Recado Bistec and Recado Negro.

Achiote, the seasoning paste used in several of the region's signature dishes, is made from annatto seeds which are found in prickly pods that grow on a tropical shrub called *Bixa orellana*. It has been around since pre-conquest days when tribesmen used it to color their skin. Today annatto is also used to make Cheddar cheese orange and butter yellow. Thanks to its increased popularity, this recado now comes in a ready-to-use liquid form. (See Resource Directory.)

While Achiote is the best known recado, many cooks say Recado Bistec, a delicious blend of spices and herbs including oregano, black pepper, garlic and cumin is the most flavorful.

The region is also associated with the "hotter-than-hell" habanero chile and the many salsas made with it, including Xni-Pec, Chile Tamulado and Ha'Si-Kil Pac. In addition to these salsas or dipping sauces, the Yucatan is noted for several cooked sauces such as its Chiltomate or roasted fresh tomato sauce, and its Kol Blanco, a type of white sauce.

Achiote or Recado Rojo
Achiote Seasoning Paste

Most modern cooks use commercially prepared achiote, either in the traditional paste form or in the new liquid version, adding cumin, oregano, salt, pepper, allspice and roasted fresh garlic, according to their taste. Some add chile for a little accent. To make it from scratch is a labor of love. Be sure to use the freshest ingredients available.

3 Tbls. annatto seeds (See Resource Directory)
1 Tbl. EACH black peppercorns, Mexican oregano, toasted and crushed
1 tsp. salt
3 whole allspice
5 cloves garlic, toasted and peeled

Bring half cup water to boil over high heat. Add annatto seeds; turn heat to low and simmer for 10 minutes. Remove from heat and let stand overnight or several hours. Drain off water and put seeds, peppercorns, oregano, salt, allspice and two or three garlic cloves in a spice grinder or mortar and pestle and grind. Add remaining garlic and a drop of water if necessary to form a paste. Store in a glass container in the refrigerator. Add mild vinegar or sour orange juice to dissolve it for a marinade.

Makes about ½ cup.

Recado Bistec
Oregano and Garlic Seasoning Paste

Despite its name, this seasoning paste is not just for beef. It is used on fish, chicken and pork as well as beef. Its distinct olive-green color comes from the fresh oregano and its heady aroma from all of the spices. I find the aroma irresistible.

¼ tsp. ground clove
1 Tbl. black peppercorns
4 whole allspice
1 cinnamon stick, about 2 ½ inches, broken into pieces
1 tsp. cumin seeds
¼ cup fresh oregano leaves, dried and crushed*
1 head garlic, roasted, peeled
½ tsp. salt
 Mild vinegar

Grind dry spices in a spice grinder or mortar and pestle until very fine. Add roasted garlic, salt and a drop or two of vinegar until it forms a paste. Store in a glass jar in the refrigerator. To use, dissolve in sour orange juice, or a combination of mild fruity vinegar, like a rice vinegar and sweet orange juice. (Use only fresh fruit juice.)

Makes about ½ cup

*Or use 1½ Tbls. toasted and crushed Mexican oregano

Recado Negro
Blackened Chile Seasoning Paste

This shiny black recado is the most difficult to make because it requires roasting chiles until they are black, a process bound to set off smoke alarms, so be prepared. Some people find that the burned chiles and abundant spices in this recado irritate the stomach, but the rich flavor does not irritate the palate. Used in several regional dishes, it is widely available in the Yucatan but not so in other parts of Mexico or abroad. Unfortunately, there is no substitute.

2 lbs. dried red chiles (chile guajillo or arbol)
1 Tbl. black peppercorns
5 whole allspice
5 whole cloves
1 tsp. cumin seeds
1 Tbl. salt
1 large head garlic, roasted and peeled
1 Tbl. Mexican oregano, toasted
1 Tbl. Achiote paste
1 tsp. mild vinegar

Wash, seed and de-vein the chiles. Pat dry and place on a hot griddle, comal, cast-iron skillet or a charcoal grill outdoors. Roast on high heat until thoroughly charred, turning from time to time and avoiding the smoke which may irritate your eyes. Soak the blackened chiles in salt water. Meanwhile, grind to a powder the peppercorns, allspice, cloves and cumin seeds in a spice grinder. Remove the chiles from the salt water and rinse off any remaining soot. Cut chiles into small pieces and combine in a food processor with the ground spices, salt, roasted garlic, oregano, Achiote and vinegar and blend to a smooth paste. Store in a jar in the refrigerator up to 1 year.

Makes about 1 cup.

Salsa de Tomate

FreshTomato Sauce

This sauce is served with a wide range of dishes. If you broil or char the ingredients and add some chile, it becomes Salsa de Chiltomate. This is so naturally sweet, so delicious and so simple, you won't be tempted to use prepared sauce.

5 Roma tomatoes, seeded and chopped
1 small white onion, chopped
1 Tbl. oil
Salt to taste

After chopping the tomato and onion, put them in a blender or food processor for about 10 seconds to liquify. (If you don't want to seed the tomatoes, chop and add them to the blender. Liquify and then strain.) Heat oil in a saucepan over medium heat; add the sauce, stir, add salt and lower the heat to simmer for 15 minutes, stirring occasionally.

Makes about 1½ cups.

Salsa de Chiltomate
Roasted Tomato and Chile Sauce

This roasted version of tomato sauce is served with Poc Chuc, eggs, Frijol Con Puerco, Papadzules or as a soup topping. The texture should be chunky.

5 Roma tomatoes, roasted
1 small white onion, roasted
1 habanero or Serrano chile, roasted
1 bunch cilantro, stems removed
Salt to taste

On a hot comal, roast the tomatoes, chile and onion; seed and partially peel the tomatoes and the chile. (Use rubber gloves to protect your hands with the chile.) Leave some of the charred peel on for flavor and rustic appearance if you wish. Chop the onion and cilantro. Combine tomato, chile and onion in a molcajete and grind or mash the ingredients together; or mix in a food processor or blender for just a few seconds. Don't over-blend; the sauce should be chunky.

Mix in chopped cilantro by hand and add salt to taste. Reheat before serving if you wish. (It can be served hot or at room temperature.)

Makes about 1 cup

Xni-Pec

Tomato, Onion and Habanero Chile Salsa

This is Yucatan's version of salsa cruda, the ubiquitous fresh tomato salsa served with almost everything. In Mayan it means "nose of the dog." You can make it as hot as you like by increasing or decreasing the chiles. You can even cheat by using serrano chiles until you work up to habaneros. But the real secret is the sour orange juice.

3 tomatoes
1 to 2 habanero chiles
5 Tbls. cilantro leaves
1 small red or white onion
½ cup sour orange juice, limon or mild vinegar
Salt to taste

Seed and finely chop the tomatoes and chiles. Feel free to use as little as ¼ to ½ of a habanero. They are potent and there's no point making a salsa so hot you can't enjoy it. Mince the cilantro leaves and onion and combine with tomatoes and chile in a bowl. Add sour orange juice, limon or vinegar and salt to taste. Let the salsa rest for at least an hour before serving.

Makes 1 cup.

Chile Tamulado
Broiled Habanero Salsa

From the word "tamul", which is Mayan for molcajete — the basalt mortar and pestle used in Mexico — comes the word "tamulado" or mashed. You can use the blunt end of a knife and a small bowl to achieve more or less the same result. This fresh habanero salsa, also called Chile Kut, is served in many restaurants and found in most homes. A fire-eaters favorite, it is always served on the side, thank heaven. Some say the addition of a roasted and mashed garlic clove helps prevent gastric disruptions.

5 habanero chiles, charred or broiled
¼ tsp. salt
Juice of sour orange, limon or enough mild vinegar to form a salsa

After you char the chiles on a comal over high heat, or next to the flame on a gas burner, mash them in a small bowl or molcajete with salt and sour orange juice, limon or enough mild vinegar to form a salsa. Add roasted and mashed garlic if you wish and use with extreme caution.

Makes about ½ cup

Ha'Si-Kil Pac
Tomato and Toasted Pumpkin Seed Salsa

Experience a little gastronomic time travel when you taste this dip made with indigenous ingredients. Use it with tortilla chips, pita chips or fresh vegetable crudites. It is often served with Lebanese "crack bread," a toasted and puffed pita bread covered with sesame seeds. The toasted, puffed bread is "cracked" open with a rounded fist to create lots of dipping chips.

4 Roma tomatoes
1 small habanero chile
1 cup (about ½ lb. or 250 g.) toasted, ground pumpkin seeds*
½ small red onion or a bunch of cebollina, chopped
Juice from sour orange, or half sweet orange and half mild vinegar
Small bunch cilantro
½ tsp. salt

Blacken the tomatoes and a habanero chile on a griddle, comal or in a cast-iron skillet over medium-high heat. Seed and chop tomatoes and put them in a blender or processor and blend for about 30 seconds. Add ground pumpkin seeds, chopped onion or cebollina and a little juice. Blend to a chunky paste, along with cilantro leaves, a piece of habanero chile and salt. Process or blend to a chunky dip, adding more juice as needed. Taste and adjust seasonings if necessary. Be careful not to use too much habanero until you taste the mixture, because the heat varies.

Makes about 1½ cups.

*Toast hulled green seeds in a dry skillet on medium heat for about 15 minutes. Grind in a spice grinder or food processor. 3 cups whole seeds equal about 1 cup ground.

Kol Blanco
White Sauce

This rich and creamy sauce is used with poultry, fish and other dishes, including Queso Relleno.

2 Tbls. oil
¼ cup minced onion
1 xcatic or guero chile
1 tomato, seeded and finely chopped
2 cups broth (depending on the recipe)
1 cup milk
⅓ cup wheat or masa flour
5 stuffed olives, chopped
5 to 10 capers, depending on size, chopped
1 Tbl. EACH chopped raisins, almonds
Salt and pepper to taste

In a large, non-stick skillet heat oil over medium-high heat and saute the onion and chile xcatic. Leave the chile whole and be careful it doesn't break open. Add the chopped tomato and continue to saute, 3 to 5 minutes. Add strained broth; bring mixture to a boil and lower heat. Whisk milk and flour together until smooth and add slowly to the simmering mixture. Add remaining ingredients. Return to a boil, lower heat and simmer for about 10 minutes. Taste and adjust seasoning if necessary.

Makes about 3 cups

Recado Escabeche
Mild Pickling Spice

In making most escabeche dishes, we generally add the seasonings individually, but you can premix and add them all at once. In the Yucatan, of course, you can buy the seasoning already blended and then add an extra dash of pepper, cinnamon, clove, oregano or cumin to your taste.

10 peppercorns or 1 tsp. freshly ground black pepper
¼ tsp. EACH cinnamon and ground cloves
2 tsps. toasted and crushed Mexican oregano leaves
2 bay leaves
½ tsp. ground cumin or ¾ tsp. toasted cumin seeds

Grind all of the ingredients, except bay leaves, together in a spice grinder, minichopper or mortar and pestle. Add whole bay leaves. Store in a jar with an air-tight lid.

Makes a scant ¼ cup.

Recado de Papadzules
Pumpkin Seed Paste for Papadzules

This lovely green recado is used for making Papadzules. It is available from spice venders in the municipal mercados and at supermarkets at certain times of the year.

12 to 16 oz. green hulled pumpkin seeds
1 stalk epazote
¼ white onion
½ head garlic
2 cups salted water or chicken broth (2 tsps. salt)

Slowly toast pumpkin seeds in a dry skillet or on a baking sheet on low heat. Meanwhile, in a saucepan, bring epazote, onion and garlic to boil in salted water or broth on high heat for about 5 minutes. In a blender or food processor, grind the toasted seed. Strain about ¼ cup boiled liquid into the ground seeds to form a paste, reserving the rest of the water. Take the paste out of the blender or processor and work it by hand in order to extract a teaspoon or so of oil to be used as a garnish.

To make the sauce, return paste to blender or processor and gradually add the rest of the water or broth. In a non-stick frying pan, heat the sauce over very low heat until it thickens to a creamy texture.

Makes about 2 cups.

Fritanga
Sauteed Onion, Tomato and Bell Pepper

Like the Cajuns of New Orleans, Yucatecans begin most of their traditional soups, stews and main dishes with a medley of sauteed vegetables. Cajuns use onion, bell pepper and celery, a mix they reverently call the Holy Trinity. In the Yucatan, tomatoes replace the celery to complete the trio. While neither a sauce nor recado, Fritanga is included here because it is an essential building block that adds depth and dimension to innumerable main dishes and soups. The tomatoes are always meaty Romas and the onions are always white.

1½ tsps. oil
1 medium garlic clove, minced (optional)
½ small white onion, minced
¼ green bell pepper, minced
2 Roma tomatoes, seeded and minced*

Heat oil in a medium-sized skillet over medium-high heat. Add garlic and stir for a few seconds; add the onion and continue stirring until onion is translucent. Add the pepper, stir and add the tomatoes. Lower the heat and saute for about 3 minutes. Add to soups, stews, sauces as directed, or as you wish

*Depending on the recipe, the tomatoes may require peeling.

Crema de Ajo
Creamy Garlic Dip

Along with eggplant dip and garbanzo bean dip, this recipe of Lebanese origin is available commercially, but the homemade version is far superior. Serve it with vegetable crudites, or toasted pita bread chips. Many people make this dip with vegetable oil, but I prefer it with olive oil, which has its own rich flavor and texture. You can use half vegetable and half olive if you wish.

1 egg plus 1 or 2 egg whites at room temperature
1 Tbl. white onion, chopped (optional)
2 medium cloves garlic, chopped
1 tsp. fresh lemon or lime juice
¼ tsp. Worcestershire sauce
½ tsp. salt or more to taste
2 cups light olive or vegetable oil

Put the egg and egg white(s) in a blender along with the onion, if using, and garlic. Blend well. Now, with the blender running, remove the center cup from the lid and pour in the lemon juice and Worcestershire sauce and salt. Now, slowly pour in the oil in a steady stream like you would to make mayonnaise. Continue pouring until the mixture is almost stiff. Taste and add more salt if desired. Continue to blend until mixture is stiff.

Makes 2 cups.

Beans, Rice and Pasta

Beans, like corn tortillas, are an integral part of the Yucatecan diet, served for breakfast, lunch and dinner, with eggs, meat, fish and poultry. My friend and teacher Adelida Kantun once told me that a meal without beans is "muy triste," very sad.

As in Cuba and many Caribbean countries, black beans are the legume of choice. They are served as an entree or side dish, whole or pureed, and as an appetizer, spiced and refried. White beans, red beans, garbanzos, lentils and two seasonal favorites – espelon and ibes – are also popular.

Neither rice nor pasta are indigenous to the region, but since the 16th century arrival of the Spaniards these grains have come to play a major role in everyday cooking. Rice is always prepared pilaf style and seasoned with either onion, garlic, tomatoes, bouillon or the cooking liquid from black beans.

It's amazing how pasta has wound its way around the world into so many cuisines. The smallest corner "tienda" and the largest mega-markets in the Yucatan, all have pasta sections. The favorite seems to be fideo, whether it is used in soup or mixed with rice in the popular Arroz Con Fideo, a traditional side dish served with Puchero.

Frijol Kabax
Black Beans

The "x" is pronounced with a "sh" sound, as if it were kaBASH. This is black beans at their most basic, the starting point for other bean dishes. The beans are left whole and served in their cooking liquid, like a soup, to accompany main courses. Add bits of meat, such as pork, ham, bacon, chorizo, longoniza or any type of smoked sausage for extra flavor.

1 lb. black beans, pre-soaked*
1 tsp. salt
¼ white onion, chopped
1 stem epazote, if available
1 xcatic chile, roasted
1 tsp. cumin
1 tsp. toasted and crushed oregano

Rinse and pick over the beans. Put them in a medium-sized pot with 2 quarts water. Bring to a boil over high heat, add salt, onion and epazote. Cover and simmer over low heat for 30 minutes. Add the whole roasted chile, the cumin and crushed oregano and continue to simmer on low 30 minutes more or until tender, adding more water as needed. Test for tenderness and add more salt, if desired. Use beef or chicken broth instead of water, if you wish, to enrich the flavor. Remove the chile if it breaks open.

Serves 6.

*If you forget to pre-soak the beans overnight, bring water to a boil, add beans and let them soak one hour; drain and begin again with fresh water.

Frijol Colado
Strained Beans

This soupy dish is the typical accompaniment to Poc Chuc, many egg dishes, Pescado Frito and Cochinita Pibil. It is also the starting point for refried black bean dip. Remember when cooking beans don't add salt until beans boil and the skins begin to soften and break open. Also, don't put all of the cooking liquid in at once; use enough to cover at first and add as needed.

1 lb. black beans, pre-soaked
1 stem epazote, if desired
½ tsp. salt
1 Tbl. lard or vegetable oil
1 habanero or xcatic chile, whole
¼ white onion, sliced

Put the beans in a large pot with water to cover, a stem of epazote, if desired. Bring to a boil on high heat, covered; lower the heat. Add more water as needed and simmer, covered, on low heat about 1 hour. Test for tenderness, add salt and continue simmering until tender. When tender, liquify the beans in a blender or food processor with some of the cooking liquid. Push the pureed beans through a strainer, adding more liquid as needed. Return strained beans to the pot and simmer, UNCOVERED, until they are the consistancy of a cream soup.

In a small frying pan, over medium heat, saute the whole habanero (don't let it break open) and the onion slices in lard or vegetable oil for about 5 minutes. Add this to the beans and bring to a boil over high heat. Lower the heat and simmer, adding water if you wish, for about 5 minutes. Be careful the chile doesn't break open. The whole chile adds flavor and a slight piquancy; but it will not burn unless it is cut open and spills out its hot seeds. You can serve the chile separately for those who like to fire up their appetites. Ladle beans into individual soup bowls and serve.

Serves 8 to 10.

Frijol Refrito
Refried Black Beans

Refried beans are an excellent side dish as well as one of the most popular appetizers in the Yucatan. This recipes is for an attractive party dish that is both whimsical and delicious. Serve it plain as a side dish with eggs, pork, ham or just spread it on a warm corn tortilla for a simple and nourishing snack.

2 cups Frijol Colado or 2 cans refried beans*
2 Tbls. lard or oil
¼ white onion, chopped
1 habanero, xcatic or guero chile
Salt to taste
Onion, cilantro, tomato slices, chips and crumbled dry cheese for garnish

Heat a tablespoon of the lard or oil in a medium-sized non-stick skillet over medium-high heat and saute the onion until it is golden. Add the chile, being careful it doesn't break open. Let it flavor the onion and lard for about 2 or 3 minutes and remove. Add the Frijol Colado (see recipe) or canned beans and saute until they begin to dry, adding lard or oil as necessary to prevent the beans from sticking to the skillet. Taste and add salt as desired.

For a botana, continue stirring until the beans are dry enough that you can roll them over into a log with a spatula. Mound the refried beans into a log or football shape on an oblong plate and garnish with tortilla chips until it resembles a porcupine. Add thinly sliced onion, cilantro, crumbled dry cheese and surround the bean dip with tomato slices. For a more contemporary treatment, serve the beans warm, surrounded by crumbled blue cheese, with a basket of warm chips for dipping.

Serves 6.

*You can use whole canned beans too. Just puree them in a blender or food processor along with their liquid and run them through a strainer.

Frijol Con Puerco
Black Beans With Pork

My friend Candy Mendez once began a story by saying, "It was a Monday. I remember because we were having Frijol Con Puerco." In Yucatan the two are synonymous. The bigger the pot the better.

1 lb. black beans
1 lb. boneless pork loin or shoulder
1 sprig epazote
½ onion, sliced
Salt
Arroz Blanco or Arroz Negro
Salsa de Chiltomate
Garnishes:
4 radishes, chopped
¼ red onion, chopped
2 limes, quartered
Small bunch cilantro, stemmed and chopped
Avocado, peeled and chopped into small cubes
½ kilo tortillas (20 or more)

Put beans in a large pot with a quart of water and bring to a boil over high heat. Remove from heat and let sit for an hour, or soak beans overnight. Drain and rinse the soaked beans. Put beans in a large pot with 2 quarts water and bring to boil over high heat. Reduce heat and simmer on low heat, covered for about 1 hour. Meanwhile, rinse pork and cut into 2 inch cubes. Add to beans along with epazote, onion and salt and continue cooking over medium heat, covered for another hour. Test the beans for tenderness and the broth for flavor. Add salt as desired and more water if necessary. While pork and beans are cooking prepare the rice, salsa and garnishes.

For a colorful presentation put the rice in the center of a large serving dish surrounded by individual mounds of minced radish, red onion, cilantro, quartered limes and chopped avocado. Put the pork and beans in another serving bowl or soup tureen. Yucatecans usually put the pork and beans on top of the rice and top that with Chiltomate. Then they add their favorite garnishes and a squirt of lime juice. However, some prefer to eat the rice and pork on a plate, with the beans and broth in a cup or bowl on the side, with their favorite garnishes. Serve warm corn tortillas on the side.

Serves 6.

Tortitas de Frijol
Fried Black Bean Patties

These little patties are also known as Negritos and Gorditas. They make great appetizers that can be eaten by hand as well as with a fork.

1 lb. fresh tortilla dough (masa)
1 to 2 tsps. salt
3 Tbls. liquid lard or oil
1 cup cooked, well-seasoned black beans

To the tortilla dough, add salt and lard or oil and blend well. Drain the beans and reserve some of the liquid. Mash the beans a bit with a fork and blend into the tortilla dough. Add some bean liquid if the masa is dry. Form into small patties for appetizers, or larger patties for an entree and fry in oil in a large heavy skillet over medium-high heat. Drain on paper towels and serve topped with Chiltomate, a dash of crema and a cilantro leaf or a few sprigs of cebollina (like chives).

Makes 15 to 20 patties, depending on size.

Arroz Rojo
Tomato Flavored Rice

This is not the so-called "Mexican rice" commonly served on combination plates at Mexican restaurants North of the boarder, but rather a version of rice pilaf. It is only faintly red (rojo) from the fresh tomatoes.

1 clove garlic
1½ tsps. oil
¼ small white onion
1 large or 2 medium Roma tomato
½ tsp. salt
1 cup rice
2 cups water

Crush the garlic and saute in oil in a medium sauce pan over medium-high heat. Thinly slice the onion; seed and chop tomato and add both to garlic. Rinse and drain rice and add to sauteing vegetables. Add water and salt. Cover, bring to a boil and simmer on very low heat about 15 minutes.

Serves 4 to 6.

Arroz Negro
Black Rice

Made with the cooking water from black beans, this dish is traditionally served with Frijol Con Puerco. But it can be made anytime you have cooking water from black beans available. It adds a dramatic note to a number of dishes, and is especially complimentary with grilled fish and pork.

1 cup rice
1½ tsps. oil
¼ small white onion, finely chopped
1 clove garlic, finely chopped
2 cups black bean cooking liquid
Salt to taste

Rinse and drain the rice. Heat oil in a heavy saucepan over medium-high heat. Add onion and garlic and saute until the onion turns transparent. Add the rice and saute until it turns golden. Add the black bean broth and bring to a boil; add salt to taste, cover and simmer on very low heat for 15 minutes.

Serves 4 to 6.

Arroz Blanco
White Rice

Plain, boiled white rice is never served in the Yucatan. All rice is made pilaf style, by first sauteeing onion, garlic or tomato. The Mediterranean influence is most evident. Even potato lovers like this rice. It has enough flavor to be eaten by itself.

1 clove garlic, mashed
1½ tsps. oil
¼ small white onion, minced
1 cup rice
2 cups water with chicken bouillon* or chicken broth
½ tsp. salt

Heat oil in a medium non-stick saucepan on medium-high heat and add the garlic. Saute a minute or so; add the onion and continue sauteing for a few minutes. Rinse and drain rice and add to saucepan. Stir the rice to coat it with oil. When it begins to take on a little golden color, add water or broth and salt. Cover, bring to a boil, turn heat to low and simmer about 15 minutes. The rice is ready when the liquid is absorbed and air holes form at the top.

Serves 4 to 6.

*Chicken bouillon is used extensively as a flavor enhancer in rice, soup, even vinaigrette.

Arroz Con Fideo
Rice With Pasta

Yucatecans serve this with Puchero. We like it with pork, chicken and all by itself. It ranks right up there with mashed potatoes as the quintessential comfort food. (Some have been known to eat the leftovers cold, right from the refrigerator, when no one is looking.)

1 large or 2 small cloves garlic, roasted
¼ white onion, roasted
½ Tbl. olive oil
1 cup rice
½ cup fideo, broken into small pieces
2 cups chicken stock, or water and 2 tsps. chicken bouillon
1 tsp. salt or to taste
¼ tsp. Condimento or imitation saffron
1 Tbl. chopped cilantro

Heat oil in a saucepan over medium-high heat; add the rice and fideo and saute until the fideo starts to brown. Peel and chop the roasted garlic and onion and add to rice and fideo; add stock, condimento, and salt to taste. Cover, bring to boil, and simmer over low heat and until liquid is absorbed, about 10 minutes. Sprinkle on fresh cilantro.

Serves 6 to 8.

Ensalada de Macarrones
Macaroni Salad

Isn't it amazing how pastas of all shapes and sizes have wound their way around the world and into the cooking pots of so many cultures. This salad appears frequently at potlucks, picnics and family gatherings throughout the region. Chunks of pineapple are a sweet, pleasant surprise.

1 lb. coditos (elbow macaroni)
1 tsp. salt
½ cup fresh or frozen peas, blanched
¼ lb. ham cut in small chunks
½ cup pineapple chunks (canned)
1 tsp. Black pepper
¼ lb. Monterey Jack or mild Cheddar cheese, cubed
½ cup Mexican media crema or sour cream
½ cup mayonnaise or salad dressing
¼ cup minced parsley

Boil 2 quarts of water in a medium sauce pan on high heat; add salt and macaroni; stir. When water returns to the boil, lower heat and simmer about 7 minutes. Meanwhile, blanch the peas for a few minutes in boiling water and drain them. Drain and rinse macaroni with cold water. In a large bowl, mix pasta with remaining ingredients except parsley. Garnish with minced parsley.

Serves 8.

Pastel de Lujo
Layered Rice Casserole

Experienced cooks devised this recipe as a delicious way to use leftover rice and/or picadillo. But it is just as good when you make it from scratch.

4 cups cooked rice (2 cups uncooked)
3 cups creamed corn
2 eggs
4 Tbls. Butter
1 tsp. salt
Picadillo:
1 Tbl. oil
2 large garlic cloves, chopped
1 lb. EACH ground pork, beef
1 small onion, finely chopped
1 medium bell pepper, seeded and finely chopped
4 Roma tomatoes, seeded and finely chopped
1 Tbl. capers, chopped
2 Tbls. raisins, chopped
½ tsp. cinnamon
¼ tsp. EACH ground allspice and clove
Salt and pepper to taste

Put the rice in a large mixing bowl. In a blender, puree the creamed corn along with the eggs butter and salt. Pour mixture over rice and blend well. Set aside.

For the Picadillo: Heat oil in a large, heavy-bottomed skillet and brown the garlic, pork, beef and onion over medium-high heat. Add the bell pepper and tomatoes and continue to cook over medium heat. Add remaining ingredients and simmer about 10 minutes until the flavors are well blended. Taste and add seasoning if needed.

Put half the rice and corn mixture into a 9-by-13-inch buttered casserole. Add the picadillo filling and cover with remaining rice mixture. Bake for 45 minutes in a 350-degree oven.

Serves 8.

Poultry

Pit-roasted turkey (Pavo Pibil) was one of the first meals the Maya served to the Spaniards upon their arrival in the early 16th century, according to Bishop Diego de Landa who wrote an extensive chronicle of the conquest period. He noted that the merchant class liked to entertain lavishly, spending large sums on their banquets.

Centuries later, the mid-19th century explorer and writer John L. Stephens also tells us about the delicious pit-roasted turkey served to him by the hospitable Maya.

Although the breed of turkey has changed over the centuries and the modes of preparation have evolved and expanded, turkey remains a regional favorite. Poultry farming is big business, but many people in the small villages still raise their own turkeys on the back patio for "noche buena," Christmas Eve, dinner. Turkey is also served on special occasions such as birthdays, weddings and anniversaries.

While turkey is the bird of choice for special occasions, chicken plays a prominent role in the day-to-day menus of most Yucatecans. Prepared in countless way with various recados and other condiments, it is perhaps best known in the region's famous Pollo Pibil. In this dish, chicken is basted with Achiote, wrapped in a banana leaf and baked. Regional specialties found in other chapters, such as Sopa de Lima, Panuchos, Tamales Colados and Mucbipollo, are also chicken based.

Pollo En Achiote
Grilled or Broiled Chicken With Achiote

You can use a whole chicken or chicken parts for this recipe. It looks as delicious as it tastes. Serve it with cole slaw, potato or macaroni salad, or Yucatecan style with pickled red onions, warm corn tortillas and habanero hot sauce.

1 whole chicken cup up or equivalent part
2 large cloves garlic
½ tsp. Mexican oregano
½ small white onion
1 tsp. salt or chicken bouillon
½ ounce Achiote dissolved in sour orange or mild vinegar*

Rinse the chicken and place it in a stew pot with the garlic, oregano and onion and enough water to almost cover. Bring to a boil on medium-high heat, covered; lower heat, add salt and simmer for about 10 minutes. Remove chicken. Strain broth and reserve for another use. Rub the chicken with Achiote. Prepare a grill or broiler and brown the chicken on medium high heat, 10 to 15 minutes.

Serves 4 to 6.

*Or use ¼ cup liquid Achiote

Pollo En Fideos
Chicken With Noodles

You could call this chicken noodle soup, but that would be the ultimate in understatement, especially for those who grew up on the canned variety. Actually, the dish can be as soupy as you want it to be. Hearty, healthy, homey, it will sooth and satisfy your appetite if not your soul.

1 large chicken, cut up (about 3 lbs. or 1½ kilos)
½ head garlic, roasted
½ medium white onion
1 tsp. chicken bouillon
½ tsp. roasted and crushed Mexican oregano
1½ tsp. oil
1 Roma tomato, minced
½ small white onion, minced
¼ green bell pepper, minced
2 stems flat-leaf parsley
2 stems cilantro
8 oz. fideo (small, fine noodles)
Salt to taste

Rinse chicken and put it in a large pot with enough water to cover, along with the roasted garlic, onion and oregano. Bring to a boil on medium-high heat, lower the heat, add bouillon, cover and simmer about 20 minutes.

Heat the oil in a medium skillet over medium-high heat and saute the minced tomato, onion and bell pepper for about 5 minutes. Add to the simmering chicken along with the parsley and cilantro, tied together.

Meanwhile, in the same skillet, saute the fideo in a little oil on medium-high heat until it turns golden. Add browned fideo and some salt or chicken bouillon to the chicken and vegetables. Bring to a boil, lower the heat, cover and simmer until the fideo is cooked, about 5 minutes. Add more water if you prefer a soupier dish.

Serves 6.

Pollo Adobado
Achiote Seasoned Chicken With Potatoes

An old standby, this popular home-style dish is also made with pork.

1 whole chicken cut up, or equivalent parts
2 oz. (about ½ small box) Achiote
Juice of 3 to 4 sour oranges (1 cup) or half sweet orange and half mild vinegar
Salt
½ tsp. EACH black pepper, cumin, oregano
1 bell pepper
1 white onion
2 cloves garlic
3 tomatoes
1 Tbl. oil
2 large or 4 medium potatoes
2 xcatic (guero or banana) chiles
Banana leaf (or aluminum foil)
¼ cup chopped cilantro leaves

Rinse and cut chicken into serving size pieces; remove skin, if you wish. In a large dish or bowl combine Achiote, sour orange juice, salt, pepper, cumin and oregano. Mix well to dissolve the Achiote; add chicken and stir to cover all of the parts with the marinade.

Meanwhile, seed, core and thinly slice the pepper; chop the onion, tomato and garlic. Peel, quarter and slice potatoes into wedges and set aside in a bowl of water (to prevent discoloration). In a Dutch oven heat the oil over medium-high heat and saute peppers, onion, tomato and garlic for about 5 minutes. Add the chicken and its marinade, the whole xcatic chiles and cover with a piece of banana leaf or aluminum foil. (The banana leaf helps seal in the juices while the chicken cooks and adds a little flavor, but it is not essential.)

Let the meat simmer, covered, on medium heat for about 30 minutes. Add potatoes and continue cooking another 15 minutes. To serve, remove banana leaves, pour into a serving dish and sprinkle with cilantro.

Serves 6.

Pollo Alcaparrado
Chicken With Capers and Olives

Mayan and Mediterranean ingredients blend beautifully in this personal favorite, combining raisins, capers and olives with sour orange and yellow xcatic chiles.

2½ to 3 lbs. chicken, cut up
½ Tbl. Recado Bistec
Juice of 2 sour oranges, about 1 cup
2 xcatic or guero chiles
1 whole (small or medium) head garlic
1 small white onion, thinly sliced
1 small green bell pepper, seeded and thinly sliced
½ Tbl. oil
1 large Roma tomato, chopped
1 tsp. salt
¼ tsp. freshly ground black pepper
¼ tsp. cumin
1 Tbl. capers
2 Tbls. raisins
8 olives, seeded and sliced
½ Tbl. chicken bouillon
Pinch saffron or Condimento Espanol

Rinse chicken and rub it with Recado Bistec dissolved in a little sour orange juice. On a griddle or comal over high heat, roast chiles and whole garlic until charred; set aside. Saute onion and bell pepper on medium heat in a non-stick skillet with some of the oil. Add chopped tomato and continue to saute. In a stew pot, heat remaining oil on medium-high heat and brown the chicken. Add sauteed vegetables. Cut garlic in half crosswise, removing most of the charred papery husk. Add to the pot along with chiles. Stir and cook over medium heat. Add salt, remaining sour orange juice, pepper, cumin, capers, raisins, olives, bouillon and saffron; stir. Cover and continue cooking on low for 15 minutes, or until chicken is fully cooked. Be sure to taste the chiles and remove if they are too hot. If you want more broth, add a little water. Serve with white rice and garnish with cilantro leaves.

Serves 4 to 6.

Pollo Pibil
Achiote-Basted Chicken Wrapped in Banana Leaves

Achiote and banana leaves point up the Mayan origin of this popular dish, first cousin to Cochinita Pibil. The word pibil comes from pib, which means pit, or an underground oven lined with rocks. This technique is still used in some villages, but oven baking is the norm for city dwellers.

1 large chicken cut up or 6 legs
2 Tbls. Achiote
Juice of 2 sour oranges, or ½ cup EACH sweet orange and vinegar
½ tsp. EACH cumin, black pepper
1 tsp. EACH salt, oregano
Banana leaves or aluminum foil
1 sprig epazote, if available
2 large cloves garlic, roasted and mashed
2 Roma tomatoes, sliced in rounds
1 medium onion, sliced in rounds
1 bell pepper, sliced in rounds
¼ tsp. chicken bouillon
Cilantro garnish

Cut chicken into serving size pieces and pierce all over with the tip of a sharp knife. Dissolve Achiote in sour orange juice. Add cumin, pepper, salt and oregano and mix to blend evenly. Line a 9-by-13-inch baking dish with banana leaves or aluminum foil, making sure there is enough overhang to fold back over the top. Arrange chicken pieces in the pan and pour Achiote marinade over them. Be sure each piece is well coated. If available, put an epazote leaf on each piece of chicken. Put some mashed garlic, sliced tomato, onion and pepper on each piece. Sprinkle some chicken bouillon on top. Fold the excess portions of banana leaf or foil over the top and tuck down into the pan, making sure the dish is well sealed so the meat doesn't dry out in the oven. (You can also wrap each piece individually.) Bake at 375-degree for 1 to 1½ hours. Fold back the banana leaves or foil and let the chicken brown on top for 10 minutes at 450 degrees. Sprinkle with fresh chopped cilantro leaves and serve with Frijol Colado, Cebolla Encurtida and fresh corn tortillas, or white rice and a green salad.

Serves 4 to 6.

Puchero de Gallina
Chicken and Vegetable Stew

This is one of three versions of Puchero, a favorite Sunday dish to serve the whole family, and anyone else who might happen to drop by. Other versions call for pork and beef as well.

1 large chicken cut up
2 tsp. salt
1 whole head garlic, roasted
1 tsp. Recado Bistec
¼ cup sour orange juice, or mild vinegar
½ tsp. immitation saffron or Condimento
1 sprig mint
1 small calabasa Yucateca (pattypan squash), peeled, seeded and halved
1 large chayote squash, peeled, seeded and halved
2 or 3 large potatoes, peeled and quartered
1 or 2 turnips, peeled and quartered
1 or 2 medium carrots, peeled and chopped
1 plantain, peeled and cut into large chunks
1 cup garbanzo beans, pre-cooked or soaked
 Arroz con Fideo:
 2 cloves garlic, roasted
¼ white onion, roasted
 1 Tbl. oil
 1 cup rice
½ cup fideo, broken into small pieces
2 tsp. chicken bouillon
¼ tsp. condimento espanol or pinch saffron
Chopped cilantro
Salsa de Rabano:
 6 to 8 radishes, washed and minced
½ small red onion, minced
 1 whole habanero chile, if desired
 1 bunch cilantro, minced
½ cup sour orange juice, or use ½ sweet orange and ½ mild vinegar
Salt to taste

> > > > >

Puchero continued

Rinse chicken and cut into serving size pieces, with or without skin. Put it in a large stew pot with enough water to cover and bring to a boil on medium-high heat. Lower heat and add salt and roasted garlic.. Dissolve recado in sour orange juice and add to pot. While the chicken cooks, wash and prepare the vegetables and add them according to their cooking time, carrots and squash first, then the turnip and potatoes, plantain, and the squash blossoms last. If the garbanzos are NOT pre-cooked, add them first, but be sure to soak them first. When the vegetables are tender, remove them from the pot to prevent overcooking, and keep them warm.

For Arroz con Fideo: Heat oil in a saucepan on medium-high heat and saute the rice and fideo until the fideo starts to brown. Chop the roasted garlic and onion and add to rice and fideo; add about 2 cups water, bouillon and, condimento or saffron. Cover, bring to boil and simmer over low heat until liquid is absorbed.

For Salsa de Rabano: Mix all ingredients and let stand at least 1 hour to enhance the flavor.

To serve: Arrange vegetables on a large serving platter with the rice and fideo in the middle, sprinkled with chopped cilantro. Serve meat and broth in soup bowls with salsa on the side. Diners add salsa, vegetables and rice to their soup bowls at their own pace and to their own taste.

Serves 6.

Pollo Ticuleño
Chicken Ticul-Style

Named for the city Ticul, this recipe is adapted from a book of authentic regional recipes. Another perhaps more popular version calls for breaded fried chicken breast served between crisp tortillas with fried bananas alongside — who can say which is the definitive one.

1 whole chicken cut up, or equivalent parts
3 cloves garlic
1 tsp. EACH oregano, salt
1 Tbl. Recado Bistec
½ cup sour orange juice or mild vinegar
2 large potatoes, peeled, washed and chopped
4 to 5 slices thick meaty bacon or ¼ lb. ham, chopped
1 large white onion, thinly sliced
½ green bell pepper, thinly sliced
1 large lettuce or cabbage core, chopped (optional)
2 Tbls. oil

Rinse and parboil chicken with garlic, oregano and salt in a large stew pot over medium-high heat for about 10 minutes. Remove, drain and rub with the Recado Bistec dissolved in vinegar or sour orange juice, along with some of the chicken broth. Set aside to marinate. Meanwhile, prepare the vegetables for sauteing and set aside. Be sure to cover the potatoes with water so they don't discolor.

Heat oil in a heavy skillet on medium-high heat. Drain chicken parts, reserving the marinade, and brown in oil. When well-browned, remove chicken to a plate and keep warm. Add the chopped potatoes to the skillet and brown well. Remove and keep warm with the chicken. If using bacon, drain off any oil in the pan and fry the bacon until crisp on medium heat. Otherwise brown the ham in the oil. Remove bacon or ham and saute the onion, pepper and lettuce or cabbage core in remaining fat. Add reserved potatoes and bacon or ham to skillet along with remaining marinade. Place chicken parts on top, cover and simmer on medium heat for 5 minutes. Remove the lid and continue to simmer another 5 minutes to reduce liquid. Serve with warm tortillas or French bread and a green salad.

Serves 4

Pollo en Escabeche de Valladolid
Valladolid-Style Chicken With Pickled Onions

This version of escabeche comes from Valladolid, in the eastern part of the state of Yucatan. You can make this dish in advance and then just before serving, reheat the broth and broil the precooked chicken a few minutes until golden brown.

1 large chicken cut up, or equivalent parts
2 tsp. chicken bouillon
Olive oil
2 Roma tomatoes, chopped
½ bell pepper, chopped
1 medium white onion, chopped
1 head garlic, roasted
1 large or 2 medium red onions, quartered and roasted
4 xcatic or guero chiles, roasted
2 habanero chiles, if desired
½ tsp. Mexican oregano, salt
¼ tsp. EACH cumin, black pepper
1 bay leaf
3 or 4 mint leaves
1/4 tsp. clove
½ cup juice from sour orange, or half sweet orange and half mild vinegar
2 Tbls. Recado Bistec

Put a quart of water, or chicken broth, in a stew pot and bring to a boil. Clean and cut chicken into serving pieces and add to pot along with bouillon. When it returns to a boil, lower the heat, cover and simmer. Heat olive oil in a non-stick skillet on medium-high heat and saute the tomato, pepper and onion; add this *fritanga* to the pot. Roast the garlic, quartered red onions and whole chiles. (Don't let the chiles split and spill their hot seeds.) Add to stew pot. Add oregano, cumin, black pepper, salt, bay leaf, mint leaves and cloves. Simmer until chicken is just barely cooked, about 20 minutes. Remove chicken and cool. Add ¼ cup sour orange juice to broth. When cool enough to touch, rub chicken parts with Recado Bistec dissolved in remaining sour orange juice or vinegar. Brown them under a broiler for 10 to 15 minutes, until golden brown. Ladle broth over browned chicken and top with roasted red onions and xcatic chiles.

Serves 4 to 6

Poc Chuc de Pollo
Marinated Chicken Cutlets

In the Mayan language, poc chuc means roasted on a charcoal grill. Many people think it means pork because the recipe is commonly used for pork. Hacienda Teya makes a nice version of Poc Chuc de Pollo, which it serves cut up on a bed of pickled red onions.

1 lb. boneless chicken breasts
3 Tbls. sour orange juice, or half sweet orange and half mild vinegar
½ Tbl. Recado Bistec
Pinch freshly ground black pepper
1 tsp. salt
1 roasted garlic clove, mashed
1 tsp. toasted crushed oregano

Rinse and pound the cutlets with a wooden mallet. Dissolve the Recado Bistec in the sour orange and put it in a bowl with the chicken. Add the remaining ingredients and stir to blend the flavors. Let the chicken marinate about 15 minutes. Drain and cook cutlets on a grill or griddle over medium heat until well browned on both sides, 2 to 3 minutes per side. Serve with pickled red onions (Cebolla Encurtida), Roasted Tomato Sauce (Chiltomate), rice, and black beans. Fire-eaters might also add a little dish of Chile Tamulado or Xni-Pec.

Serves 4.

Pollo en Jugo de Naranja
Chicken in Orange Juice

Some have suggested that this dish is an adaptation of the French duck l'orange. Whatever its origin, it was the first regional recipe that I learned to make. It continues to be a favorite. Be sure to use freshly squeezed orange juice. It makes a difference.

2 ½ to 3 lbs. chicken, cut up
½ tsp. freshly ground black pepper
Salt to taste
1 small head of garlic, roasted, peeled and mashed*
3 Valencia or similar oranges, juiced (about 1½ cups)
3 large Roma tomatoes
½ white onion
1 small red or green bell pepper
¼ cup olive oil
1 Tbl. EACH raisins, capers
10 stuffed or pitted green olives, sliced

Rinse the chicken parts; sprinkle with salt and pepper and marinate with the orange juice and mashed garlic. Meanwhile, cut the tomatoes, onion and pepper into ¾- to 1-inch chunks. Heat the olive oil in a heavy-bottomed skillet over medium-high heat and saute the vegetables 2 to 3 minutes. With a slotted, remove vegetables to a Dutch oven or stew pot and add the orange juice marinade, raisins, capers and olives. Cover and keep warm over very low heat. Drain chicken and brown in the same skillet over medium-high heat. When well browned, add to Dutch oven and simmer, uncovered, about 20 minutes on low heat. Deglaze any browned bits in the skillet with some of the marinade juices and add to the simmering pot. Serve with white rice or boiled new potatoes and a steamed green vegetable or a salad of fresh greens. After soaking dry garbanzos, rub them between the palms of your hands to remove the skins before cooking.

Serves 4 to 6.

*Roast the whole unpeeled head on a comal, in a dry cast-iron skillet or under a broiler. When well charred, squeeze the cloves out of their skin and mash with a fork.

Pavo or Pollo en Relleno Negro
Turkey or Chicken With Black Stuffing

This is one of the classic dishes found on menus at regional restaurants. Unlike stuffed turkey served at Thanksgiving in the United States, this turkey is cooked on top of the stove. It is a favorite at village celebrations and one of the dishes craved by homesick Yucatecans working and living away from home. The negro refer to the use of Recado Negro used in the stuffing (relleno).

1 large whole chicken or small turkey
¼ white onion, cut in strips
¼ red or green bell pepper, cut in strips
1 tomato seeded, cut in strips
Oil
1 small head garlic, roasted
½ tsp. ground cumin
1 tsp. oregano, roasted and crumbled
1½ oz. Recado Negro
Salt
2 Tbls. flour
<u>Relleno (Stuffing):</u>
5 eggs, 3 hard cooked
¼ white onion
¼ red or green bell pepper
1 garlic clove
Oil
1 lb. ground pork
Salt
1 oz. Recado Negro
½ cup flour
½ tsp. ground cumin
½ tsp. ground oregano
Cheesecloth

> > > > >

Relleno Negro continued

Rinse and cut the chicken or turkey into serving pieces and set aside. Heat oil in a large stew pot or Dutch oven on medium-high heat and saute the chopped onion, pepper and tomato. In the meantime, char the whole garlic on a comal or griddle over high heat until blackened. In a blender or food processor, dissolve Recado Negro with a cup or more of water. Strain it through cheesecloth into the pot. Add another cup of water to pot and bring to a boil; add chicken pieces, whole roasted garlic, cumin and oregano. Return to boil; lower heat to simmer for 1 to 1½ hours, depending on the size of the chicken or turkey. Test the broth and add salt if desired. Dissolve flour in some water and add to the broth to thicken.

For the relleno: Mince onion, chile and garlic and saute in oil on medium-high heat in a medium skillet. Add ground pork and saute over medium heat until no longer pink. Peel the hard-cooked eggs. Remove the yolks; keep them whole and set aside. Mince the egg whites and add them to the pork mixture, along with salt and the two raw eggs. Dissolve about 1 tsp. Recado negro in 1 Tbl. water and add to the mixture along with remaining ingredients. Blend the pork filling by hand and form into a ball with the three whole egg yolks in the middle. Wrap in a cheesecloth and tie at the top. Add to the pot and simmer along with the chicken and broth. When the chicken is cooked, remove the cheesecloth-wrapped relleno. When it has cooled enough to touch, unwrap and slice the relleno. Serve with chicken, some broth and Arroz Blanco or Arroz Rojo.

Serves 12, depending on size of chicken or turkey

Pavo en Relleno Blanco
Turkey With White Stuffing and Sauce

Pavo en Relleno Blanco is similar to American-style roast turkey in that it can be stuffed and roasted. Traditionally however, it was cooked in the ground. A major difference today, is that many Yucatecans precook their poultry and then roast it for a short time just to brown it.

1 large whole chicken or small turkey
½ head roasted garlic
1 Tbl. Salt
1 tsp. EACH oregano, Recado Bistec
Relleno Blanco (Stuffing):
5 eggs, 3 hard cooked
¼ EACH white onion, red or green bell pepper
1 garlic clove
Oil
1 lb. ground pork
1 tsp. salt
½ cup flour
1½ tsps. Black pepper
½ tsp. EACH cinnamon, clove, saffron, oregano
10 EACH pitted green olives, large capers, raisins and almonds
Cheesecloth
Kol Blanco:
 2 Tbls. oil
¼ cup minced onion
 1 xcatic or guero chile
 1 tomato, seeded and finely chopped
 2 cups broth
⅓ cup wheat or masa flour
 5 EACH stuffed olives, capers, chopped
 1 Tbl. EACH chopped raisins, almonds
 Salt and pepper to taste

>>>>>

Relleno Blanco continued

Rinse and cut the chicken or turkey into serving pieces. Char the whole garlic on a comal or griddle over high heat until blackened. Meanwhile bring a quart of water to boil in a large stew pot; add chicken or turkey, whole roasted garlic, salt and oregano. Add stuffing wrapped in cheesecloth (see below). Return to boil. Lower heat and simmer for 2 to 3 hours, depending on the size of the chicken or turkey. Test the broth and add salt if desired. When no longer pink, remove chicken or turkey, rub with Recado Bistec, dissolved in a little broth, and roast at 400 degrees just until brown, about 10 minutes.

For the relleno: **Mince** onion, chile and garlic and saute in oil on medium-high heat in a medium skillet. Add ground pork and saute over medium heat until no longer pink. Add remaining ingredients. Peel the hard-cooked eggs. Remove the yolks; keep them whole and set aside. Mince the egg whites and add them to the pork mixture, along with salt and the two raw eggs. Blend the pork filling by hand and form into a ball with the three whole egg yolks in the middle. Wrap in a cheesecloth and tie at the top. Add to the pot and simmer along with the chicken and broth. When the chicken is cooked, remove the cheesecloth-wrapped relleno. When cool enough to touch, unwrap and slice the relleno.

Kol Blanco or white sauce: In a large, non-stick skillet heat oil over medium-high heat and saute the onion and chile xcatic. Leave the chile whole and be careful it doesn't break open. Add the chopped tomato and continue to saute, 3 to 5 minutes. Add 2 cups broth from stew pot; bring mixture to a boil and lower heat. Whisk flour and some broth together until smooth and add slowly to the simmering mixture. Add remaining ingredients. Return to a boil, lower heat and simmer for about 10 minutes. Taste and adjust seasoning if necessary.

To serve: Put a slice of stuffing covered with white sauce next to a serving of turkey. Some people serve a tomato sauce too, as they do with Queso Relleno.

Serves 8 - 12, depending on size of chicken or turkey.

Pavita Pibil
Achiote-Basted Turkey

The earthy flavor of the achiote marinade is surpassed only by the lovely rustic color of the turkey in this recipe. It is so easy to prepare, don't wait till Christmas to try it.

1 12-lb. turkey
1 small pkg. (about 3 oz.) Achiote
½ cup water
½ cup mild vinegar
2 cloves garlic
1 tsp. salt
½ tsp. freshly ground black pepper
¼ tsp. cumin
5 cups sliced white onions
1 tsp. toasted, crushed oregano

Rinse the turkey inside and out. Put the Achiote, garlic, water, vinegar, salt, pepper and cumin in a blender or food processor and liquify. Baste the turkey inside and out with the Achiote marinade. Mix the onions with the oregano and stuff the turkey with them. Sew up or truss turkey cavity. Cover turkey with aluminum foil and bake at 350 degrees for 3 hours. Remove the foil and let the turkey brown for another hour, uncovered. Let it cool for 20 minutes before slicing. Serve with Arroz Blanco (white rice) or Puree de Papas (mashed potatoes), and Calabasa Yucateca, or your favorite vegetable side dishes. Enjoy a glass of Chardonnay with your turkey.

Serves 12 to 15.

Pavo En Escabeche
Roast Turkey With Pickled Onions

Intensely flavored escabeche is a good make-ahead dish for parties. You can use chicken breasts as well, and serve the meat in pieces rather than shredded. Accompany with warm corn or flour tortillas, bolillos or French rolls, shredded lettuce and cilantro.

1 whole turkey breast, 6 to 8 lbs.
2 bay leaves
½ tsp. EACH oregano, freshly ground black pepper
1 tsp. salt
1 Tbl. EACH Achiote and Recado Bistec
½ cup sour orange juice or mild vinegar
4 large white onions, sliced lengthwise
½ Tbl. Oil
1 head garlic, roasted
2 xcatic or guero chiles, roasted
1 tsp. freshly ground black pepper
½ cup sour orange juice or mild vinegar
½ tsp. ground cumin or ¾ tsp. toasted cumin seeds, crushed
2 bay leaves
1 tsp. oregano leaves, toasted and crushed
Pinch of cinnamon and clove
1 tsp. salt

Rinse and quarter the breast, cut off the wings and put them all in a Dutch oven with enough water to cover. Bring to boil on medium-high heat. Add bay leaves, oregano, pepper and salt and simmer on low heat, covered about 20 minutes. Stir, continue simmering about 20 more minutes. Remove turkey parts and cool on a platter; reserve the broth. (At this point, you can refrigerate and continue the next day.) Baste turkey with recados dissolved in sour orange juice or vinegar. Roast the turkey in a 375-degree preheated oven in a shallow roasting pan 20 to 30 minutes, or until well browned. Let it cool.

Meanwhile, saute onions in a large fry pan with a little oil over medium-high heat. Add a cup of reserved turkey broth, roasted garlic, Xcatic chiles, pepper and sour orange juice and stir. Add remaining spices, stir and continue sauteing over low heat. Shred the turkey and stir into the onion mixture. (At first the onions will take up a lot of room but as they cook down you will be able to add the shredded turkey.) Cover and simmer turkey and onions together over low heat for 15 minutes. Add more broth and seasoning if needed.

Serves 8.

Pavo en Kol Indio

Turkey in Achiote-Flavored White Sauce

"Kol" is the Mayan word for sauce, and Indio refers to the use of Achiote in this dish featured at regional restaurants. It is a variation of Kol Blanco, or white sauce. Serve it with white rice and a green salad.

1 qt. chicken broth
½ small head garlic, roasted, peeled and mashed
½ small white onion, roasted
2½ lbs. (1 kilo) chicken or turkey, cut up
¼ tsp. cumin
¼ tsp. black pepper
¼ tsp. allspice
½ tsp. salt
½ tsp. oregano

<u>Kol Indio</u>
1 Tbl. oil
½ white onion, chopped
4 Roma tomatoes, chopped
1 bell pepper, seeded and chopped
1or 2 serrano chiles, seeded, de-veined and chopped
Salt to taste
½ pkg. Achiote (50 grams, about 1½-1¾ oz.)
½ cup flour
2 Tbls. masa flour mixed with water or broth

Put broth on to boil in a stew pot or Dutch oven over high heat. Meanwhile, charbroil the onion and half of garlic on a comal or griddle over high heat, until blackened. Rinse chicken and add to stew-pot. Add cumin, pepper, allspice, salt and oregano; bring to boil, reduce heat to medium and simmer. Add roasted onion and

> > > > >

Pavo en Kol Indio continued

peeled, mashed, roasted garlic; cover and cook about 20 minutes. When tender, remove meat and set aside; reserve broth. When cool enough to handle, separate chicken into bite-sized pieces. Discard skin and bones.

For the Kol: Heat oil in a skillet over medium-high heat. Add onions, tomatoes, peppers and chiles and saute 3 to 5 minutes. Dissolve Achiote in a ½ cup of reserved chicken broth and strain into frypan. Turn heat to low. Dissolve flour and masa flour in some broth and strain into pan; continue stirring and adding broth as needed. Taste and adjust seasonings if necessary. Continue stirring until it is a nice creamy consistency; add reserved chicken meat and cook until heated through, about 5 minutes.

Serves 6

Arroz con Pollo
Chicken and Rice

This popular dish of Spanish heritage has many versions throughout Latin America. In the Yucatan, the chicken marinates in Recado Bistec, giving it a delicious and distinct flavor.

2 lbs. chicken, cut up
1 tsp. oregano
1 large clove garlic
1 tsp. salt
1 tsp. chicken bouillon
2 Tbls. Recado Bistec
3 tomatoes
½ EACH medium white onion, green bell pepper
2 tsp. oil
1 cup rice
¼ tsp. saffron or condimento
2 to 2½ cups chicken broth
½ cup fresh or frozen peas
½ cup roasted red pepper strips (fresh or canned)

Rinse chicken and put it in a large stew pot with enough water to cover. Add oregano, garlic, salt and chicken bouillon; cover and bring to a boil on medium-high heat. Simmer about 15 minutes. Remove chicken and reserve broth. Cut the chicken into bite-sized pieces (removing bones if you wish) and rub with the recado dissolved in a bit of the broth. Set aside. Seed and chop the tomatoes; julienne the onion and bell pepper. Heat one teaspoon of the oil in a large skillet on medium-high heat for a few minutes. Add and saute the tomato, onion and bell pepper. Add the rice and saute until it turns golden. Put the saffron or condimento in the reserved chicken broth; add broth to the rice, cover, bring to boil and simmer on low heat. Meanwhile, saute the chicken in the remaining oil in a non-stick skillet on medium-high heat. When it is golden, add to the rice along with any pan juices. Cover and continue to simmer. When the liquid is almost absorbed, add the peas and continue cooking another 5 minutes. Garnish with red pepper strips.

Serves 8.

Pork and Beef

Because it was indigenous, and also because it was favored by the conquering Spaniards, pork figures prominently in the region's cooking. The most famous of all Yucatecan dishes is Cochinita Pibil, in which a whole baby pig is basted with achiote, then wrapped in banana leaves and baked in a pit lined with hot rocks.

American explorer and writer John Lloyd Stephens described the cooking of this dish in his seminal work on the Maya, Incidents of Travel in the Yucatan in 1843, detailing the use of Achiote, sour orange juice, banana leaves and pit roasting. Historians believe the dish actually pre-dates Columbus.

Beef came with the Spaniards and trial and error proved that the cattle best suited to the hot, humid climate are the humpbacked Brahmin variety originally from India, and also used extensively in Brazil. Although lean, the meat is tough and not as flavorful as North American beef. Regional dishes that call for ground meat usually use a mixture of pork and beef for better flavor.

Cochinita Pibil
Pork Roasted with Achiote

This pre-conquest dish is still cooked in the traditional way, in a "*pib*"or rock-lined pit in many outlying villages. But a conventional oven works just fine. You can even make it in a Crockpot! Simple to prepare, it is great for a make-your-own taco party.

2 banana leaves (or aluminum foil)
3 lbs. pork leg, loin, or shoulder well trimmed
Juice of 4 sour oranges or half sweet orange and half mild vinegar
2 to 3 oz. Achiote
¼ tsp. cumin
1 tsp. EACH oregano, black pepper, salt
1 garlic clove, mashed or pressed
2 bay leaves
<u>**Accompaniments:**</u>
Corn tortillas, or soft torta rolls
2 cups Frijol Colado or Frijol Refrito
Cebolla Encurtida (Pickled Red Onions)

Line a large baking pan with the banana leaves, leaving enough overlap to wrap over and around the pork. Cut the pork into large chunks and put it in the baking dish. In a small bowl, dissolve Achiote in sour orange juice; add remaining herbs and spices and blend well. Pour this marinade over the meat and let it rest about 1 hour. Wrap the banana leaves over the top of the pork and seal with a piece of aluminium foil. Bake in a preheated oven at 350 degrees for 1½ hours, or until it is very tender and almost falling apart.

Assembly: Using two forks, shred pork into bite-sized pieces. Spread a spoonful of strained (or refried) beans on a warm tortilla, top with shredded pork and a sprinkle of pickled red onions. Roll and place seam side down on a plate. Alternately, spread beans on a torta roll, top with pork and onions. If you wish, you can include shredded lettuce or cabbage as a topping.

Serves 6 to 8.

Lechon Al Horno
Marinated Roast Pork

We first tasted this dish at a neighbor's party, where the pork was delivered by a caterer in a galvanized portable oven that resembled a miniature coffin. Also called Lechon Horneado, as in oven-baked, this is Cuba's version of Cochinita Pibil. A similar dish is also found in the Florida Keys. Once cooked, the tender pork is pulled from the carcass and served in warm corn tortillas or on rolls with accompanying salsas.

2½ to 3 lbs. pork leg, loin or shoulder
1 cup sour orange juice or half sweet orange and half lime
½ Tbl. Recado Bistec
1 or 2 large cloves garlic, mashed
1 tsp. salt
Banana leaf or foil

Rinse the pork and puncture it all over with a fork. Place it in a baking dish or small roasting pan. Dissolve Recado Bistec in the sour orange juice. Mash the garlic with the salt and add to seasoning mixture; rub this marinade all over the pork. Let it sit for about 30 minutes. Preheat the oven to 350 degrees. Put a piece of foil (or banana leaf if available) over the pork and roast for 1 hour. Remove the foil and continue roasting for 30 more minutes, uncovered. Serve with Salsa Xni-Pec.

Serves 6 to 8.

Poc Chuc
Marinated Pork Cutlets

A certain restaurant in the Yucatan claims to have originated this dish. While the restaurant may have popularized the recipe, Poc Chuc goes way back. In Maya, the words mean roasted on a charcoal grill. It is Yucatan's version of carne asada, but with pork instead of beef. Thinly sliced pork cutlets are soaked in a well-seasoned marinade and then grilled.

1 lb. pork leg or loin, very thinly sliced
3 Tbls. sour orange juice, or use mild vinegar
½ Tbl. Recado Bistec
1 tsp. salt
1 roasted garlic clove, mashed
1 tsp. toasted crushed oregano
Accompaniments:
Salsa de Chiltomate
Frijol Refrito
Cebolla Encurtida
Tortillas

Rinse and pound the pork cutlets with a wooden mallet. Dissolve the recado in sour orange juice in a shallow bowl. Add the pork and remaining ingredients and stir to blend. Marinate 30 minutes. Cook the pork on a hot griddle or grill over medium-high heat until well browned on both sides, 2 to 3 minutes per side. Serve with Salsa de Chiltomate, Frijol Refrito, Cebolla Encurtida and fresh corn tortillas. Some people cut the cooked pork in little squares, put it in a tortilla and eat it like a taco. Fire-eaters always add a little Chile Tamulado or habanero salsa.

Serves 4.

Lomitos de Valladolid
Cubed Pork Loin With Pureed White Beans

Ibes are similar to butter beans or small fresh limas, but you can use any small white beans for this dish, which comes from Valladolid, east of Merida.

1 lb. ibes or pre-soaked small white beans (alubias)
2 lbs. boneless pork loin or filet, well trimmed
1 tsp. salt
1 stem epazote, if available
Oil
½ white onion, chopped
1 large clove garlic, minced
2 tomatoes, cropped
1 small bell pepper, chopped
1 Tbl. Achiote (or 2 Tbls. liquid Achiote)
½ Tbl. Recado Bistec
2 Tbls. sour orange juice or mild vinegar
1 tsp. salt
¼ tsp. EACH freshly ground pepper, cumin, oregano
¼ cup chopped white onion
Cilantro

Put ibes or drained, pre-soaked beans in a large pot or Dutch oven and cover with water. Bring to a boil on high heat; add epazote and salt. Lower to medium and simmer until tender, about 30 minutes. Dry beans can take up to 2 hours, depending on their age. Meanwhile, cut the meat into 1-inch cubes or smaller. Heat oil in a large skillet and saute the garlic and onion on medium-high heat for about 1 minute. Add pork and let it brown. Add tomato and bell pepper and continue to saute another 2 or 3 minutes. Dissolve the recados in sour orange juice and strain into pot; add salt, pepper, cumin, oregano. Lower the heat and continue to simmer. Add enough water to make a sauce. When the beans are tender, puree in a food processor with enough cooking liquid to make them smooth. In a saucepan on medium-high heat, saute the ¼ cup chopped onion; add bean puree and simmer on low heat. Taste and add salt and pepper to taste. Serve pork and sauce on a bed of white bean puree and top with chopped fresh cilantro leaves.

Serves 6 to 8.

Lomo Frito
Pork Medallions Yucatan Style

Here is a simple sauteed meal that you can fix in under an hour. Serve with rice or potatoes and a green salad. A crisp Sauvignon Blanc makes a nice accompaniment.

2½ lbs. (1 kg.) boneless pork leg (pierna) or loin
½ Tbl. Recado Bistec
2 garlic cloves, mashed
¼ tsp. cumin
1 tsp. salt
½ cup sour orange juice, or use mild vinegar
Oil
2 Roma tomatoes, finely chopped

Cut the loin into medallions about ½ inch thick. In a bowl, combine the Recado Bistec, the garlic, cumin and salt with sour orange juice. Add the pork and marinate in this mixture for about ½ hour. In a heavy, non-stick skillet, heat the oil on medium-high heat; add the tomatoes and simmer a few minutes. Drain pork, reserving marinade. Add to skillet and brown on both sides. Add the marinating liquid, cover and simmer over low heat until the pork is tender, about 10 minutes.

Serves 6 to 8 .

Puerco Adobado
Marinated Pork Stew With Potatoes

This easy, inexpensive meal is even better the second time around. Try cooking it in a clay pot for added authenticity. Serve with white rice.

2½ lbs. (1 kilo) boneless pork leg or shoulder
½ to 1 Tbl. Achiote
Juice of 2 to 3 sour orangesor half sweet orange and mild vinegar
1 tsp. salt
1 tsp. Recado Bistec
1 small bell pepper
1 small white onion
2 large cloves garlic
3 Roma tomatoes
4 medium potatoes
1 Tbl. oil
2 xcatic (guero or banana) chiles
Banana leaf, if available, or aluminum foil
Cilantro

Rinse and trim pork; cut into 1½-inch chunks In a large bowl, combine Achiote, sour orange juice, salt, pepper, cumin and oregano (or Recado Bistec). Mix well to dissolve the Achiote; add pork and stir to cover all of the pork with the marinade. Add a little water if necessary for full coverage.

Meanwhile core and thinly slice the pepper; chop the onion, tomato and garlic. Peel, quarter and slice potatoes into wedges and set aside in a bowl of water (to prevent discoloration). In a Dutch oven, over medium-high heat make a *fritanga* by sauteing peppers, onion, tomato and garlic in oil for about 5 minutes. Add the meat and its marinade, the whole xcatic chiles; cover with a piece of banana leaf or aluminum foil to help seal in the juices. Let the meat simmer on medium heat for about 40 minutes. Add potatoes and continue cooking, covered, another 10 to 15 minutes. To serve, remove banana leaf or foil, pour pork and potatoes into a serving dish and sprinkle with cilantro leaves.

Serves 6

Puerco En Coca-Cola
Pork Simmered in Cola

One day we had quite a bit of cola leftover from a party, so we dredged up this 1950s favorite from an old cookbook. What a delicious surprise. We savored every last bit of the sweet sauce and tangy meat. Next to mixing it with rum, this is the best thing you can do with Coke. Like most popular recipes, it has many versions. Here it is prepared in cutlets. You can also cook the pork whole and slice it just before serving.

1½ lbs. boneless pork leg, or loin, sliced into cutlets
1 tsp. freshly ground black pepper
1 clove garlic, mashed and chopped
½ tsp. salt
1 tsp. vinegar
A pinch of clove, allspice, cinnamon, cumin, salt, oregano
   (or use Recado Bistec)
2 Roma tomatoes, seeded and chopped
½ green pepper, seeded and chopped
½ onion, chopped
1 Tbl. vegetable oil
1 Tbl. mustard
1 Tbl. butter
1½ cups (12 oz.) Coca Cola

Rinse and slice the pork. Pound cutlets with a wooden mallet to flatten. Put cutlets in a bowl or baking dish and sprinkle with black pepper, chopped mashed garlic, salt, vinegar, clove, allspice, cinnamon, cumin, salt, oregano (or a little Recado Bistec dissolved in the vinegar). Mix well and marinate for about 15 minutes. Meanwhile, make a *fritanga* in a small skillet by sauteing the vegetables in oil on medium-high heat. In a Dutch oven or stew pot, heat some oil on medium-high heat and brown the pork cutlets. When cutlets begin to brown, spread each with a little mustard and butter and let them continue to cook. Add the sauteed vegetables and the Coca Cola, cover and simmer over low heat for about 10 minutes. Remove the lid and reduce the liquid a bit. Serve with rice or mashed potatoes and a salad.

Serves 4

Pibxcatic

Xcatic Chile Stuffed With Cochinita Pibil

This trendy creation blends traditional and modern in a delicious, picture-perfect dish. Roasted xcatic or guero (banana) chiles filled with cochinita pibil are placed on top of steamed chaya leaves and a pool of tomato sauce. Pickled red onions garnish the plate. Use yellow bell peppers, if you wish, for a sweet rendition.

12 large xcatic (guero or banana) chiles, roasted and seeded
2 cups cochinita pibil, shredded
6 large or 12 medium chaya leaves (substitute spinach or Swiss chard)
Cebolla Encurtida (pickled red onions)
Tomato Sauce

Roast the chiles on a grill or comal on high heat, leaving the stems on. Steam chiles in a tightly sealed plastic or paper bag for about 10 minutes. Peel off most of the charred black skin, slit open vertically, leaving stems in tact; remove the seeds and veins and set chiles aside. Warm the shredded pork in its juices and keep warm. Put chaya leaves in a steamer basket and steam over boiling water for about 3 minutes. Remove and set aside to cool.

Meanwhile, prepare the pickled red onions and the tomato sauce. Fill chiles with shredded pork. On each of six plates, put a generous pool of tomato salsa and a chaya leaf (or two), spread out on top of the salsa. Place two stuffed chiles on top of the leaf. Add a garnish of pickled red onion slices on top.

Serves 6.

Filete de Puerco en Escabeche
Marinated Pork Tenderloin

This quick and easy recipe makes a nice presentation.

10 peppercorns or 1 tsp. freshly ground black pepper
¼ tsp. EACH cinnamon and ground cloves
2 tsps. toasted and crushed Mexican oregano leaves
2 bay leaves
½ tsp. ground cumin or ¾ tsp. toasted cumin seeds
1½ Tbls. fresh sour orange juice, or sweet orange and mild vinegar
½ tsp. salt
1½ lbs. (half kilo) pork tenderloin
1 small bunch cilantro

Grind all of the spices together in a spice grinder or mortar and pestle (or use Recado de Escabeche) and combine with the sour orange juice and salt to form a paste, using a blender or food processor. Rinse the tenderloin and trim off any fat. Poke holes in the pork and rub it with the escabeche seasonings. Marinate for 30 minutes, or longer if you wish. Put pork on a rack in a roasting pan and roast at 450 degrees 20 to 30 minutes, until the meat is cooked through to 160 degrees on a meat thermometer. When meat is cooked, remove from oven, cover with foil and set aside for a few minutes. Slice the pork, sprinkled with fresh cilantro and serve with mashed potatoes or rice and a green vegetable.

Serves 4 to 6.

Puchero
Meat and Vegetable Stew

This classic dish is a Sunday favorite in Yucatan while Campeche cooks serve it on Mondays. Puchero comes in many versions: Puchero de Tres Carnes, Puchero de Gallina and Puchero Vaquero. This recipe is made with only two meats — beef and pork. Feel free to double the recipe, add chicken or turkey, and vegetables according to your liking and the season. Variations in preparation, as well as style of eating, abound. Some people like to mash the vegetables, for example.

1 lb. stew beef
 1 lb. pork leg, shoulder or loin
1 head garlic, roasted
1 tsp. crushed oregano leaves
¼ tsp. EACH freshly ground pepper, allspice, cinnamon, clove, cumin
2 bay leaves
2 tsp. chicken or beef bouillon
1 chayote squash, peeled, quartered and seeded
1 large or 2 small yams, peeled and cut into large chunks
2 carrots, scraped and cut into 2-inch chunks
1 medium Yucatecan squash (pattypan squash), peeled and quartered
½ lb. garbanzos, precooked
1 plantain, peeled and cut into large chunks
¼ to ½ head cabbage
Pinch of imitation saffron or Condimento
Salt and pepper to taste
Bouquet garni of fresh cilantro and mint, if desired
Arroz con Fideo:
2 cloves garlic, roasted
¼ white onion, roasted
1 Tbl. oil
1 cup rice
½ cup fideo, broken into small pieces
2 tsps chicken bouillon
¼ tsp. Condimento or imitation saffron

> > > > >

Puchero continued

<u>Salsa de Rabano:</u>
6 to 8 radishes, washed and minced
½ small red onion, minced
1 whole habanero chile, if desired
1 bunch cilantro, minced
½ cup sour orange juice or substitute mild vinegar
Salt to taste

While garlic is roasting, trim and cut beef and pork into chunks. Bring 1½ qts. water to boil in a large stew pot over high heat. Add beef and roasted garlic, return to the boil, lower heat and cook on medium about 20 minutes; add pork and oregano, pepper, allspice, cinnamon, clove, cumin. Stir to blend and continue cooking another 20 minutes; add yams, carrots, squash, garbanzos, plantains, cabbage and saffron. Add water if necessary. Simmer until meat and vegetables are tender. Add bouquet garni of fresh herbs and salt and pepper to taste. Remove vegetables as they become tender so they don't get mushy; set aside, keeping them warm.

For Arroz con Fideo: Heat oil in a saucepan over medium high heat and saute the rice and fideo until the fideo starts to brown. Mince the roasted garlic and onion and add to rice and pasta; add about 2 cups water, bouillon, condimento or imitation saffron. Cover, bring to boil, lower heat and simmer until liquid is absorbed.

For Salsa de Rabano: Mix all ingredients and let stand at least 1 hour.

To serve: Arrange vegetables on a large serving platter with the rice and fideo in the middle, sprinkled with chopped cilantro. Serve meat and broth in soup bowls with salsa on the side. Diners add salsa, vegetables and rice to their soup bowls at their own pace and to their own taste.

Serves 6.

Chuletas Con Cebollas y Pasitas
Pork Chops With Onions and Raisins

Sweet and savory best describes this easy-to-fix recipe gleaned from an old community cookbook put out by a private schools in Merida. Serve with rice or mashed potatoes and your favorite green vegetable or salad.

2½ lbs. (1 kilo) thin pork chops
2 cloves garlic, mashed
2 sour oranges, juiced, or half sweet orange and mild vinegar
½ tsp. EACH salt, freshly ground pepper, cumin, Mexican oregano
   (or use ½ Tbl. Recado Bistec)
2 medium white onions
Oil
½ cup raisins
White wine, if desired

Rinse the pork chops and pound them with a wooden mallet. Combine mashed garlic, juice and spices (or recado) and blend well before rubbing into the pork chops. Let the chops marinate while you dice the onions. Heat oil in a large, heavy-bottomed skillet on medium-high heat and saute the onions for 2 minutes; turn heat to low, add the raisins and simmer until the raisins plump and the onions soften, 2 to 3 more minutes. Remove and set aside. Take chops from marinade, reserving juices, and put them in the pan to brown on both sides over medium-high heat. When the chops are well browned, put the onions and raisins on top, pour on the reserved juices, adding a bit of white wine if necessary; cover and simmer over low heat for about 10 minutes. Serve with a crisp white wine such as Sauvignon blanc.

Serves 6.

Jamon Claveteado
Ham In Clove Sauce

Reminiscent of Virginia ham, this dish is popular during Christmas holidays. Serve with mashed potatoes and a vegetable of your choice.

4 lbs. boneless ham
For the marinade:
5 cloves
15 white peppercorns
5 whole allspice
1 cinnamon stick, about 2½ inches long
For the sauce:
1 cup water
1 cup sugar
3 EACH whole cloves, allspice
1 cinnamon stick, about 2½ inches long
2 bay leaves
1 cup sugar
1 cup sweet sherry

If you start with a precooked ham (jamon de pierna), rolled and boned, you can skip this first step. If you are starting with a shank or butt, cook the ham in enough water to cover with a couple of bay leaves, on medium heat for about 20 minutes per pound or until it reaches an internal temperature of 160 degrees. When cooked, remove from water, let it cool and peel off any skin or fat.

For the marinade: Grind the spices in a spice grinder. Mix them with a tablespoon of water and rub the mix into the ham, puncturing it in several places so the seasoning will penetrate. Let it sit for 30 minutes or so.

For the sauce: Put the marinated ham in a large stockpot or Dutch oven along with a cup of water, the sugar, whole cloves and allspice, the cinnamon broken up and the bay leaves. Bring the water to boil on high heat; turn heat to low and let it cook, covered, for 30 minutes, turning the ham ever 10 minutes. Pour the sherry over the top of the ham and let it simmer, uncovered, another 10 minutes basting the ham frequently with the pan juices. Remove from the pot and cut in thick slices. Serve with pan juice

Serves 10.

Albondigas con Yerbabuena
Meatballs With Fresh Mint in Broth

A popular home-style dish, this recipe is adapted from a regional cookbook.

1 lb. ground beef and pork mixed
¼ lb. boiled ham, ground
2 stems fresh mint
¼ tsp. EACH cinnamon, cumin, clove
1 Tbl. EACH capers, raisins, chopped almonds, bread crumbs
1 egg
4 tomatoes
½ onion
4 cloves garlic
Oil
2½ cups beef broth (or water and bouillon)
1 Tbl. capers, finely chopped
1 stem EACH mint, parsley
Salt to taste
2 potatoes, peeled and cubed, or 6-7 oz. (200g.) fideo pasta

In a medium-sized bowl mix the ground meat and ham. Chop mint leaves, almonds, raisins, capers and combine with meat along with, bread crumbs, cinnamon, cumin, clove and egg. Mix well with a fork, then use your hands to form large meatballs. Now make a *fritanga* by chopping the tomatoes, onion and 2 garlic cloves and sauteing them in oil over medium-high heat in a heavy-bottomed skillet. Char the remaining 2 garlic cloves over high heat. Heat broth in a Dutch oven over medium-high heat; add the *fritanga* and bring to a boil over high heat. Lower heat to medium and carefully add meatballs to broth. Simmer on low heat making sure the meatballs don't break open. Add remaining tablespoon finely chopped capers to broth. Mash the charred garlic and add to pot. Add the mint and parsley, leaves and stem. Add potatoes (or fideo) and continue simmering until meat and potatoes are fully cooked, about 10 more minutes. Serve with warm French bread, a tossed green salad and a glass of red wine.

Serves 4

Bistec de Cazuela
Seasoned Simmered Beef

Another name for this quick dish might be potted beef. Any full-flavored cut will work. Although the dish includes potatoes, it is often served with rice. In Campeche, it is a Thursday staple, while Yucatecans serve it on Tuesdays.

1½ lbs. chuck or round steak, well trimmed
1 oz. Recado Bistec, about ⅓ of a small package
Juice of 2 or 3 sour oranges, or mild vinegar and water
1 large clove garlic, crushed
½ tsp. salt
1 tsp. oil
½ red or green bell pepper, sliced
½ onion, sliced
¼ tsp. cumin
1 tsp. crushed oregano
2 tomatoes
1 xcatic or guero chile, roasted
2 potatoes

Trim and pound beef to tenderize, if necessary. In a bowl, dissolve recado with the sour orange or vinegar by rubbing it between your fingers. Cut beef in thin slices; put it in the bowl and massage recado into meat. Add crushed garlic and salt. Set aside to marinate for 15 minutes. Meanwhile, slice pepper and onion into thin strips. In a large skillet, heat oil over medium heat and saute pepper and onion until onion turns translucent. Remove from skillet and set aside. Add meat, reserving marinade. Saute meat on medium-high heat until it begins to brown; add cumin and oregano. Chop tomatoes and add to meat; saute for a few minutes. Return onion and pepper to skillet; add marinade. Rinse marinade bowl with a little water and add to skillet. Peel, quarter and slice potatoes and add to skillet. Add roasted xcatic chile. Cover and simmer on medium heat until potatoes are tender, about 10 minutes. Serve with rice, a green vegetable or salad.

Serves 4.

Carne Adobada Con Papas

Achiote Seasoned Beef With Potatoes

Similar to Bistec de Cazuela, this dish uses Achiote instead of Recado Bistec and a typical *fritanga* instead if sliced tomato, pepper and onion. Also, the potatoes are cooked separately and then sliced and added later.

1 lb. beef sirloin, chuck or round steak well trimmed
1 oz. (about 1/3 of 3 oz. package) Achiote
½ cup sour orange juice or use mild vinegar and water
½ tsp. salt
1 tsp. oil
3 Roma tomatoes
½ white onion
1 green or red bell pepper
1 xcatic chile
½ lb. potatoes

Rinse and slice the meat. Dissolve Achiote in sour orange juice or mild vinegar and salt. Set aside. Heat the oil in a large, non-stick skillet and brown the meat over medium high heat. Chop the tomatoes, onion and bell pepper and add to the skillet along with the reserved Achiote and let it cook on medium heat, uncovered for about 10 minutes. Char the xcatic chile and add it to the pan. Cover and simmer on low heat. Meanwhile, cook the potatoes. When tender, peel and slice in thick rounds. Serve beef with sliced potatoes and a green salad.

Serves 4.

Chocolomo
Beef Stew With Organ Meats

Traditionally, Chocolomo was prepared and served after a bullfight during pueblo fiestas. The word means fresh-killed loin, or meat, still warm from the kill. It calls for organ meat as well as beef. Feel free to add beef liver, heart, kidneys and brains according to your taste.

2½ to 3 lbs. stewing beef
2 to 3 cups water
1 tsp. toasted oregano leaves
1 small head garlic, roasted
1 tsp. EACH salt, freshly ground black pepper
½ tsp. cumin
½ Tbl. EACH Achiote and Recado Bistec
2 sprigs mint or cilantro
Salt to taste
Vegetables and potatoes, if desired
8 radishes, washed and finely chopped
1 small red onion, finely chopped
2 habanero chiles, finely chopped
½ cup cilantro, finely chopped
1 cup sour orange juice or half vinegar and half sweet orange juice
Salt to taste
Habanero sauce

Trim any fat or grizzle from the meat and cut into bite size pieces. Put meat in a stew pot and add water, oregano leaves, garlic, pepper and cumin. Cover, bring to a boil over medium high heat. Turn heat to low and simmer. Skim off any scum that may accumulate. Dissolve the recados in some beef cooking water and strain it into the pot. Stir and continue to simmer on low heat. Add two sprigs of mint or cilantro and salt to taste. If you wish, add some carrots, squash and potatoes after the meat has cooked about 45 minutes. Meanwhile, combine radish, red onion, habaneros, clantro and sour orange juice and let it sit so the flavors will blend. Serve the Chocolomo accompanied by the radish salsa, habanero sauce, and white rice if you wish.

Serves 8.

Beef Kibbehs
Cracked Wheat and Ground Meat Patties

Kibbehs are a Lebanese import that have taken root in the Yucatan, along with the thousands of Lebanese who migrated here in the last century. Some kibbehs are made without any meat at all. Commercial kibbehs are made into a hollow oval which is cracked open and filled with Cebolla Encurtida (pickled red onions) for a truly cross-cultural treat. Homemade kibbhes are made into patties of varying sizes. At Alberto's Continental Restaurant in Merida, the kibbehs are vary large, like a Salisbury steak.

1 cup cracked wheat
1 tsp. crushed oregano
1 tsp. salt
½ tsp. freshly ground black pepper
¼ cup finely chopped white onion
1 lb. ground beef (or lamb)
1 large clove garlic, mashed
¼ cup chopped mint leaves
Oil for frying

Bring a quart of water to boil in a covered, medium saucepan over high heat. Add the cracked wheat, turn off the heat and let it soak overnight or for a few hours before using. Drain well and squeeze out the water. In a bowl, mix the soaked wheat with oregano, salt and pepper, chopped onion, ground meat, garlic and mint. Mix well by hand. (If the mixture doesn't hold together well, add an egg.) Form into patties. Heat about ¼ inch oil in a large, heavy skillet over medium-high heat. Fry the patties until they are golden brown on both sides. Drain on paper towels and serve warm with your favorite salsa, or with a Lebanese-style salad made of chopped tomato, cucumber and onion with dressing made of plain yogurt, lemon juice and minced garlic. Accompany with pita bread.

Serves 4 to 6.

Trapo Viejo
Seasoned Shredded Beef

There are many versions of this old standby. Cubans serve it with peas and chile morron (roasted red peppers), while Yucatecans use Achiote. It is a perfect dish to make with leftover pot roast or stew of any kind, be it Yucatecan Puchero or all-American beef stew. Serve it as an entree with rice and a vegetable or use it as a filling for tacos or empanadas.

1 lb. flank steak (or leftover roasted or stewed beef)
½ tsp. crushed oregano
½ medium white onion, roasted
1 large clove garlic, roasted
Salt and pepper to taste
½ Tbl. oil
2 large Roma tomatoes, chopped
½ green bell pepper, chopped
½ medium white onion, chopped
1 serrano or xcatic chile, if desired
1 sour orange
1 piece of achiote paste, about an inch around
Beef broth

Rinse and trim meat. Put 1 quart of water in a stew pot on high heat. Add crushed oregano, roasted onion and garlic. Cut meat in large chunks and add it to the water. Cover, bring to a boil, lower heat and simmer until the meat is good and tender, about 1 hour, depending on the meat. Remove meat and set broth aside. When meat is cool enough to touch, shred it into pieces along the grain.

Heat oil in a non-stick skillet on medium-high heat. Add the chopped tomato, bell pepper, onion and whole xcatic or serrano and saute on medium for a few minutes. Peel and squeeze the sour orange into a bowl. Dissolve Achiote in the sour orange juice and add it to the simmering vegetables. Cook over low heat for about 15 minutes. Add shredded beef to sauteing mixture, along with some of the reserved broth and let it simmer, covered, for about 20 minutes on low. (You can precook and shred the meat ahead of time, and then add it to the *fritanga* as directed.) Serve with white rice cooked with any remaining beef broth, and a salad.

Serves 4.

Queso Relleno
Edam Cheese Filled With Picadillo

According to culinary legend, Queso Relleno was created in the 1950s to honor visiting Dutch royalty, thus the use of Holland's most famous cheese. A 3-inch square is cut out of the top of a 4½- to 5-pound Edam cheese ball, which is then hollowed out and stuffed with Picadillo. The cheese is then steamed and served with two sauces. In this recipe, instead of hollowing out the cheese round, we wrap sliced Edam around the filling. It is easier and less expensive. This very rich dish is best served with a simple green salad and a glass of red wine.

5 hard-cooked eggs
1 tsp. oil
1 large clove garlic, mashed
¼ white onion, chopped
¼ red or green bell pepper, chopped
1 tomato, chopped
¼ tsp. salt
1 lb. EACH ground pork, ground beef
½ tsp. freshly ground black pepper
¼ tsp. EACH ground cumin, cinnamon, clove
½ tsp. EACH salt, crushed oregano
6 stuffed olives, chopped
10 large or 20 small capers, chopped
2 Tbls. raisins, chopped
2 raw eggs
3 Tbls. flour
½ kilo (1¼ lbs.) Edam cheese, thinly sliced
1 large or 2 small banana leaves
Cheesecloth or clean tea towel
Kol Blanco
Salsa de Tomate

Queso Relleno continued

Heat oil in a large skillet and saute mashed garlic, chopped onion, bell pepper, tomato and salt over medium high heat. Add meat and gradually stir in the pepper, cumin, cinnamon, clove, salt and oregano while the meat browns. Add the remaining ingredients and simmer about 5 minutes. Drain the mixture in a colander and reserve the broth for the white sauce. Put the picadillo in a bowl and mix in the raw eggs and flour. Chop whites of the hard-cooked eggs, keeping the yolks whole. Add chopped whites to picadillo.

Spread the cheesecloth or tea towel on a large plate or counter top and crisscross two banana leaves on top, making sure you have enough coverage for the cheese-wrapped picadillo. (Cheese won't stick to the banana leaves.) Lay the cheese slices out in an overlapping circular pattern from the center. (Any extra scraps of cheese can be added to the white sauce.) Encase each egg yolk with a portion of the picadillo using all of the picadillo, and place on top of the cheese slices in a circular mound. Add extra slices of cheese to cover the top of the mound. Bring the banana leaves up over the top of the mound and then the cheesecloth; tie at the top. Put about an inch of water in the bottom of a steamer or large pot that can hold a rack or upside down dinner plate. Put wrapped mixture on rack or plate. Bring water to boil in covered pot on high heat. Turn to low heat and steam for 1 hour — Or bake in a water bath (Put one baking pan inside a larger pan and pour boiling water in the outer pan about halfway up) in a pre-heated oven at 350 degrees for1 hour, or until the cheese is smooth. Meanwhile, prepare the Kol Blanco and Salsa de Tomate and keep them warm.

To serve, unwrap the stuffed cheese and let it cool a few minutes. Slice like a pie and put each serving on a bed of white sauce, with tomato sauce on top, or put the sauces side by side.

Serves 6.

Zic de Venado
Shredded Pickled Venison (or Beef)

This classic regional dish dates back to pre-Hispanic times when deer, turkey, iguana and rabbits roamed the peninsula. Now deer are endangered, so unless you are a hunter, or have friends in high places, you will have to substitute beef. Zic de Venado can be used as a filling for tacos, and it also makes a refreshing main course salad. Make it with meat from a leftover roast, freshly grilled, braised or stewed meat. In this recipe, we stewed the meat and then used the cooking water to make soup with fideo.

1 lb. stew beef
1 tsp. salt
1 tsp. crumbled Mexican oregano
2 cloves garlic, peeled
10 to 12 radishes
½ red onion
1 bunch cilantro
1 cup sour orange juice or mild vinegar and sweet orange juice
Shredded lettuce
Sliced avocado

Put the meat in a stew pot and cover with water. Bring to boil, covered, over high heat, add salt, oregano and garlic. Turn heat to low and simmer 45 minutes to an hour or until the meat is tender when tested. Meanwhile, clean and mince the radish, onion and cilantro leaves and toss them in a large bowl with sour orange juice. When meat is tender, remove to a plate and cool, reserving broth for soup. Shred meat and add to minced vegetables and stir to blend. Refrigerate for a couple of hours and serve on a bed of shredded lettuce, garnished with sliced avocado. Accompany with warm tortillas and black beans in their own broth or fideo in beef broth.

Serves 4 to 6

Filete de Res Entomatado
Beef in Fresh Tomato Sauce

Here is one of those dishes with an earthiness that speaks to all of us. You can use the same recipe with pork or chicken and be just as satisfied with the results. Feel equally free to expand or contract the recipe according to your needs.

2 lb. tender, lean beef, thinly sliced
2 cloves garlic, mashed
1 oz. Recado Bistec
6 large Roma tomatoes
Oil
¼ EACH green bell pepper, large white onion, chopped
1 tsp. crushed oregano
Cilantro for garnish

Rinse the beef and cut it into medallion-size pieces; put it in a bowl to marinate with the garlic and Recado Bistec dissolved in a little water. Let it marinate while you prepare the tomato sauce by bringing some water to boil in a Dutch oven over high heat and submerging tomatoes for about 1 minute. Once blanched, remove from the water, peel, cut and seed them over a strainer, reserving the juices.

Heat a little oil in a large skillet over medium-high heat; add the beef and any accumulated juices; saute for a few minutes, then lower the heat and simmer. In a separate skillet, saute the pepper and onion on medium-high heat in a little oil; add them to the simmering meat. Put the tomatoes and all their juices in a blender and liquify. Add them to the simmering beef. Taste the sauce and add salt as needed. Add the oregano; continue to simmer for 30 minutes, longer if the beef is tough. When tender, serve the beef with tomato sauce and sprinkle with chopped cilantro. Accompany with white rice, a green vegetable or salad and a glass of Cabernet or Merlot.

Serves 8.

Milanesa
Breaded Pork Cutlets

There is nothing Yucatecan about this international favorite. But it qualifies for inclusion because of the unique way it is prepared and eaten, Lebanese style with pita bread.

1 lb. pork cutlets, sliced very thin
1 medium lemon or lime
½ tsp. EACH salt, pepper
1 large garlic clove, mashed
2 large eggs
1 cup bread crumbs, plus 1 Tbl. flour
2 Tbls. oil
6 medium pita bread rounds
3 medium tomatoes, seeded and chopped
1 cucumber, peeled, seeded and chopped
½ red or white onion, chopped
1 cup mayonnaise or plain yogurt mixed with marinade
Lettuce leaves
Habanero salsa

Rinse and pound the cutlets. Squeeze the lemon or lime juice into a medium bowl, mix in the salt, pepper and mashed garlic. Add the pork and marinate for 20 minutes, reserving marinade. Put the eggs in a large bowl and beat them till frothy. Put the bread crumbs and flour on a large plate or platter and mix them. Heat the oil in a large non-stick skillet on medium-high heat. Dip the cutlets in the egg and then the bread crumbs; pat and turn to fully coat with bread crumbs. Fry in oil until golden brown on both sides. Set aside and keep warm.

Meanwhile, slit open the pita rounds and warm them on a comal or in a toaster oven on medium-high heat. Prepare the vegetables; mix the mayonnaise with the leftover marinade and put it in a serving dish. Pass the milanesas on a platter with the warmed pita bread. On another plate put the chopped vegetables and lettuce leaves, and let everyone make his own pita sandwich. If you wish, add some habanero salsa.

Serves 6.

Puerco al Horno con Ciruelas Pasas
Roast Pork Loin With Prune Butter

Delicious and attractive, this dish requires a little advance preparation, but it is well worth the effort of planning ahead. Serve with a crisp white wine such as Sauvignon Blanc.

2½ to 3 lbs. boneless pork loin or filet
1½ Tbls. Recado Bistec
½ bottle dry white wine
3 to 4 oz. pitted prunes, chopped
2 Tbls. butter
3 large cloves garlic, mashed
½ tsp. pepper
1 tsp. salt

Rinse the pork and poke with the tip of a sharp knife so the seasoning can penetrate the meat. Dissolve the recado in half of the wine and pour over the meat. Let the meat marinate 3 to 4 hours, turning frequently to ensure even marination. Meanwhile, re-hydrate prunes in remaining wine.

In a food processor, puree prunes and wine with butter, garlic, pork marinade juices, salt and pepper. Put the meat in a baking dish and spread the prune butter over it. Make sure the meat is well covered. Roast in a preheated oven for about 1¼ hours at 375 degrees, covered with aluminum foil. Slice and serve with pan juices along with mashed potatoes, rice or oven-roasted potatoes. A sauteed medly of chayote squash and carrots seasoned with Mexican oregano, or blanched broccoli sauteed in olive oil with garlic and diced, roasted red peppers are nice accompaniments.

Alternate version: Butterfly the meat, marinate and then spread the prune butter inside. Roll it up, jellyroll-style and fasten with string. Roast according to preceding directions. This makes a nice presentation when sliced. Serve hot from the oven, or cold for summer buffets.

Serves 6.

Seafood

Like a big thumb, the Yucatan Peninsula juts north into the Gulf, pointing to the United States Gulf Coast. With nearly 1,000 miles of shoreline, including the Caribbean coast, the region has long enjoyed the bounty of the seas, be it squid, crab, octopus, shrimp, lobster, shark, grouper, snook, perch and mackerel.

For the ancient Maya, seafood was considered a high-status food enjoyed in great variety and abundance by elite males, according to historian Sophie Coe in her book, America's First Cuisines. Inland Maya traded game and fruit from their orchards for salt and fish from the coastal Maya.

Today fish is relatively inexpensive, especially for coastal dwellers. Certain species such as octopus are very affordable in season — August till December — while shellfish tends to be a special occasion food. Some of the seafood preparations, such as Tikin Xic — grilled (or baked) grouper or snapper basted with Achiote and sour orange, and wrapped in banana leaves — are distinctly Mayan. Others, like Pompano En Escabeche, are of Spanish origin. Seafood is also popularly served in salads and cocktails.

All along the northern Gulf Coast, visitors will see signs advertising "pescado frito," (fried fish) sold by the kilo or in individual portions. Although deep-fried, pescado frito is not battered. Nor is it served with tartar sauce or vinegar, but with pickled onions and corn tortillas – a thrifty snack that is more commonly purchased at roadside stands than prepared at home.

Fish kibbehs are another uniquely local snack. Of Lebanese heritage, they are served in many seaside restaurants, along with a typically Mayan salsa made with habanero chiles.

Camarones Asados
Grilled Shrimp With Achiote

Don't try to outshine the shrimp in this delicious dish, just provide a nice foil with well-prepared rice and a simple salad topped with sliced avocados.

1 lb. large raw shrimp (16 - 18 count) peeled and deveined
2 oz. liquid Achiote or 1 oz. Achiote paste and 1 sour orange
1 large clove garlic, roasted and mashed
¼ tsp. EACH cinnamon, clove, black pepper, cumin
1 tsp. olive oil
1 tsp. salt
1 Tbl. cebollina (chives or scallions), finely chopped, or cilantro leaves

If the shrimp is frozen, defrost in 1 qt. water with 1 Tbl. salt for about 30 minutes. The salt will make them nice and plump. Put Achiote (liquid or paste dissolved in sour orange juice) in a large bowl. Add mashed garlic, cinnamon, clove, pepper, cumin, olive oil and salt; stir to blend. Add shrimp to marinade mixture, stirring to make sure all of the shrimp are well covered. Marinate 30 minutes to 1 hour. Prepare a grill or broiler. Put shrimp on skewers or in a wire basket for grilling. Cook on medium-high heat about 2 minutes on each side or until cooked through. Don't overcook. Serve shrimp on a bed of rice and sprinkle with chopped chives or cilantro.

Serves 4.

Camarones Al Coco
Coconut Shrimp

You will find this thoroughly modern dish in trendy restaurants all along the Gulf and Caribbean coasts of the peninsula. Be sure to make the compote in advance. Coconut Shrimp can be served as an appetizer, luncheon entree or main course with rice and a salad or vegetable. A fruity white wine is a good accompaniments.

Apple Compote (make ahead):
3 tart apples
½ cup sugar
1 small stick cinnamon
Batter:
8 oz. (200 grams) flour
2 eggs
¼ tsp. salt
¼ to ½ cup milk
1½ cups crushed cornflakes
1½ cups shredded sweetened coconut
Shrimp:
2 dozen medium (21-25 count) shrimp, about 1 lb.
½ cup fresh lime juice
1 Tbl. salt
1 qt. water
Oil

For the Apple Compote: Peel, core and quarter the apples and put them in a covered saucepan with the sugar, cinnamon and a little water and cook over medium heat until soft and thick, almost like applesauce.

For the Batter: Mix the flour and egg in a bowl; add a pinch of salt and enough milk to form a thick batter. Mix the shredded coconut and crushed cornflakes together on a large plate..

>>>>>

Camarones Al Coco continued

For the Shrimp: Peel and clean the shrimp, but leave the tails on. Split the shrimp open along the inside curve from tip to tail. Put lime juice and salt in a 1-quart bowl of water. Place the shrimp in this acidulated salt water for half a minute. Drain and then dip each one first in the batter and then in the coconut and cornflake mixture. Heat the oil in a deep, heavy skillet or deep fryer on medium-high heat. and fry the shrimp, taking care not to let them get too dark.

To serve: Arrange shrimp on each plate in a flower pattern around a center portion of apple dipping sauce.

Serves 4 to 6.

Camarones en Vinagreta
Shrimp Cocktail

You can serve this dish with Xni-Pec, the Yucatan's version of Pico de Gallo, or with the salsa ingredients in individual bowls, as described in the recipe. It is a delicious first course or botana to serve with a refreshing drink on the terraza.

1 pound (16 count) large shrimp or prawns
½ tsp. oregano
½ lime
½ cup extra virgin olive oil
¼ cup white wine or sherry vinegar
1 cup EACH chopped cilantro leaves, white onion, tomato
¼ cup chopped serrano or habanero chile

Bring a quart of water to boil in a medium saucepan on medium-high heat. Add the shrimp, unpeeled, oregano and lime and cook about two minutes. Turn off the heat and let the shrimp steep until the water cools. Peel the shrimp, clean and butterfly if you wish, leaving the tails on. Put four shrimp on each plate and drizzle with olive oil and vinegar and a sprinkling of cilantro leaves. Serve the chopped cilantro, onion, tomato and chile in individual bowls to be passed.

Serves 4.

Mac-Cum de Pescado
Fish Simmered in Seasoned Broth

Almost any kind of firm white fish can be used in this recipe. Because grouper is plentiful in the Gulf, it is used most often. Swordfish steaks are also a good choice.

2 lbs. firm white fish cut in steaks
½ Tbl. EACH Achiote and Recado Bistec
½ cup sour orange juice or half sweet orange and half mild vinegar
1 tsp. crushed Mexican oregano
Pinch freshly ground black pepper
¼ tsp. cumin
1 medium white onion
1 medium green pepper
3 tomatoes, chopped
Olive oil
¼ cup minced parsley
Salt

Rinse the fish and place it in a deep skillet or Dutch oven along with a marinade made by dissolving the recados in sour orange juice. Sprinkle fish with oregano, pepper and cumin and marinate 10 minutes. Meanwhile, julienne the onion and green pepper. Heat a little olive oil in a medium size fry pan and briefly saute the onion, pepper and chopped tomatoes on medium-high heat. Add fritanga to the marinating fish along with half of the parsley and salt to taste; bring to a boil on medium-high heat; cover and simmer for 30 minutes on low heat, or until the fish is cooked through. Sprinkle with remaining parsley before serving. Serve with white rice.

Serves 4 to 6.

Chilpachole de Mariscos
Seafood Stew

Many variations of this rich dish can be found along the Gulf Coast. This one is adapted from a local community cookbook, Entre el Mar y la Milpa. If lobster is available, by all means add it to the pot. Use whatever is fresh and available, including fish heads to enrich the broth. Serve with fresh tostadas or fried tortillas, a green salad and a glass of Sauvignon Blanc . (If you have any leftovers, serve over white rice.)

1 lb. EACH, octopus, stone crab claws
2¼ lbs. (1 kilo) shrimp or lobster
1 tsp. Mexican oregano
1 Tbl. mild vinegar
3 Roma tomatoes
½ medium white onion
1 small green bell pepper
1 xcatic or guero chile
1 large clove garlic
2 or 3 ancho chiles
1 Tbl. olive oil
2 bay leaves
¼ tsp. each cumin, black pepper, ground clove, salt
1 bunch cilantro
¼ cup chopped white onion
1 lime cut up

Rinse and clean the seafood, removing as much skin as possible from the octopus. Put the seafood in a stew pot and cover with water. Add oregano and bring to a boil over medium-high heat. Lower the heat and simmer, covered about 5 minutes. Remove shrimp, crab and lobster and set aside to cool. Add a fish head if you have one, vinegar and more water if needed to cover. Return to boil, cover and simmer the octopus on low heat. Meanwhile, remove meat from shellfish and return shells to broth to enhance the flavor. Continue cooking, about 40 minutes, until octopus is tender. Remove and set octopus aside to cool, reserving broth.

>>>>>

Chilpachole de Mariscos continued

On a comal or in a dry cast-iron skillet, roast the tomatoes, onion, garlic, bell pepper and xcatic chile over high heat. When the vegetables are blackened, peel the tomatoes, garlic and bell pepper; put them in a blender along with the onion and puree them. (Set aside the xcatic chile). Put the roasted, pureed vegetables in a large deep skillet or Dutch over and set aside.

Meanwhile, wash, seed and de-vein the anchos and put them in a small saucepan; cover with water and bring to a boil over high heat; simmer on low heat 15 to 20 minutes. Drain the chiles; put them in the blender with ½ or ¾ cup reserved seafood broth and liquify. Combine the pureed chiles with the vegetable sauce and simmer over low heat. Strain reserved seafood broth into mixture and add bay leaves, cumin, pepper, clove and salt. Cut up the octopus and add it to the mixture. Taste and adjust seasoning as needed. Add shell fish, cut to bite size, and continue to simmer about 5 more minutes on low heat, just until the shrimp, crab and lobster are heated through. Chop the cilantro and put it on a plate along with the chopped onion and lime wedges and serve on the side, or garnish each bowl with some cilantro, onion and a lime wedge. Serve with a basket of tostadas (crisp fried tortillas) or French bread.

Serves 4 to 6.

Kibbehs de Pescado
Fish and Cracked Wheat Patties

Made the same way as beef kibbehs, Kibbehs de Pescado are often served as appetizers at seafood restaurants along the Yucatan coast. Use any mild white fish such as grouper (mero) or snapper.

1 cup cracked wheat
1 tsp. dried oregano
1 tsp. salt
½ tsp. freshly ground black pepper
¼ cup finely chopped white onion
1 lb. fish filets, finely chopped
1 large clove garlic, finely chopped
¼ cup chopped mint
Oil

Bring a quart of water to boil and add the cracked wheat. Turn off the heat and let it soak overnight or for a few hours before using. Drain well in a colander and squeeze out the water by hand. Add oregano, salt and pepper, chopped onion, fish, garlic and mint. Mix well by hand. If the mixture doesn't hold together well, add an egg or two. Form into patties. Heat about ¼ inch oil in a large heavy skillet over medium-high heat. Fry the patties until they are golden brown on both sides. Drain on paper towels and serve warm with your favorite salsa or with a salad made of chopped tomato, cucumber and onion with a yogurt, lemon and garlic dressing.

Makes 8 to 12 patties depending on size.

Note: If you want to make very finely ground kibbehs, run the wheat and fish through a food processor for a few seconds.

Albondigas de Pescado
Fishballs in White Sauce

This rich and delicate recipe, adapted from a community cookbook, has become one of our favorites. It takes a sure, light hand to make it, because the fish balls are very delicate and can break apart easily. The sauce must be watched too, so it doesn't burn.

1 lb. fresh filets or 1½ lbs. whole, cleaned fish
½ tsp. toasted and crushed Mexican oregano
1 large garlic clove
½ bell pepper, finely chopped
1 tomato, seeded and finely chopped
¼ to ½ white onion, finely chopped
¼ cup minced fresh mint
¼ tsp. toasted and crushed Mexican oregano
½ tsp.EACH dried parsley, white pepper
1 tsp. salt
2 eggs
¼ cup flour
Kol Blanco

Bring about a quart of water to boil in a medium saucepan. Add fish, the ½ tsp. oregno and garlic and simmer over medium heat about 10 minutes. Remove fish, reserving the broth. Let fish cool while you prepare the chopped vegetables. When cool enough to handle, squeeze all the liquid out of the fish and shred it into tiny bits. Be sure to pick out any bones. In a medium-size bowl, mix the fish with the minced vegetables, herbs, salt, pepper, eggs and flour, using a wooden spoon. Form into 1- or 1½-inch balls.

For the Kol: Follow recipe for Kol Blanco using reserved fish broth, but leave out the milk, raisins and almonds. When the mixture starts to bubble, add salt and pepper to taste. Add the fish balls, one at a time with a spoon. Don't stir them because they are very delicate and break apart easily. When sauce returns to the boil, lower heat and simmer for 10 to 15 minutes, covered on a very low flame. Be careful not to burn the sauce. Garnish with fresh parsley. Serve on a bed of rice accompanied by a green salad or vegetable.

Serves 4

Filete de Mero Arrollado
Stuffed Grouper

Many seafood restaurants offer some type of rolled and stuffed grouper. The fish is often filled with a seafood mixture in a white sauce, then breaded and deep fried. This version is healthier and easier to prepare for home cooks. You can use chaya in the filling as well.

12 small fish filets (grouper, or other mild white fish)
Juice from 1 small lime
½ tsp. EACH salt and freshly ground black pepper
1 large clove garlic, mashed

Rinse the filets and marinate them in the lime juice, salt, pepper and garlic

Filling:
¼ bell pepper
¼ medium white onion
1 carrot
1 tomato
1 small potato or a piece of squash
Oil
Salt and pepper to taste

Breading:
1 cup bread crumbs
2 Tbls. flour
3 eggs

Garnish:
Parsley
Slices of lime

>>>>>

Filete Arrollado continued

For the filling: Mince the bell pepper, onion, carrot, tomato and potato. (Use whatever vegetable you have on hand or prefer, including spinach or chaya.) Saute the vegetables in a little oil over medium-high heat about 5 minutes or until tender. Add salt and pepper to taste..

For the breading: Mix breadcrumbs and flour on a dinner plate or in a glass baking dish. In a small bowl, beat the eggs until nice and light.

Assembly: Put a tablespoon of sauteed vegetables at one end of each filet, roll it up and fasten with a piece of toothpick if necessary. (If you have some filling leftover, use it in soup.) Dip the rolled filets in the beaten eggs and then dredge in breadcrumbs, patting the crumbs into the fish. Place the filets on an oiled baking dish and bake for 15 to 20 minutes at 350 degrees. Garnish with chopped fresh parsley and sliced limes. Serve with white rice and a green salad.

Serves 4.

Pan de Cazon
Stacked Tortillas With Black Beans and Shredded Baby Shark

This classic dish from Campeche is an excellent way to use leftover fish. In place of the cazon or baby shark (called dogfish in some areas) use any mild-flavored fish. In some versions, the tortillas are stuffed with refried beans, like Panuchos. In this recipe, the beans are simply spread on top of the tortilla.

16 corn tortillas
1½ cups or 1 can refried black beans
Cazon filling:
1 Tbl. corn oil
2 leaves of fresh epazote, if desired
½ white onion finely chopped
½ lb. grilled cazon or other leftover fish, shredded
2 small tomatoes, seeded and finely chopped
Salt to taste
Tomato sauce:
1 lb. tomatoes
1 Tbl. oil
1 white onion finely chopped
2 leaves of fresh epazote, if desired
Salt and white pepper to taste
Garnish:
4 habanero chiles, if desired
1 avocado

Cazon filling: In a medium-sized non-stick pan, heat the oil on medium-high heat; add the onion and saute until transparent. Chop the epazote and add to pan along with shredded cooked fish and chopped tomatoes. Add a bit of salt and continue cooking for 3 to 4 minutes, or until cooked through and all of the liquid is gone.

>>>>>

Pan de Cazon continued

Tomato sauce: Put the tomatoes in a medium-sized sauce pan and cover them with water. Bring to a boil on high heat. Reduce heat and simmer until skins begin to crack and pull away from the flesh, about 10 minutes. Drain and puree in a food processor or blender. In a large non-stick pan, heat the oil and cook the chopped onion over medium heat until transparent. Finely chop the epazote and add to the onion along with pureed tomatoes. Continue cooking on medium heat until the sauce thickens a bit. Season to taste with salt and pepper.

Assembly: Warm the fresh corn tortillas on a hot comal or griddle. Put one tortilla on each of four plates and spread some refried beans on each; sprinkle some prepared cazon filling on each. Repeat with two more layers of tortillas, beans and cazon and top each with a final tortilla. Pour tomato sauce over each stack and garnish each with a habanero and two slices of avocado.

Serves 4.

Pulpo En Su Tinta
Octopus in Its Own Ink Sauce

Getting the ink out of the octopus for this dish is no small task. It's actually easier and less messy to cut it out while the pulpo is frozen. Easiest of all, of course, is to have your friendly fishmonger do it for you.

2½ lbs. (1 kilo) octopus with its ink sac intact
1 tsp. EACH oregano, salt
4 Roma tomatoes
1 large white onion, halved or two small onions
1 small bell pepper
2 cloves garlic
1 Tbl. olive oil
3 to 4 bay leaves
1 tsp. EACH cumin, salt
½ tsp. oregano
Pinch cinnamon, clove, freshly ground black pepper and allspice
Mild vinegar or juice of sour orange
Cilantro

If the octopus is not cleaned, make a cut in the head, turn it inside out and remove the innards. Carefully cut open the stomach and cut out the ink sac, taking care to keep the sac intact. Dissolve ink sac in a small bowl with a little vinegar and water. Discard the remaining viscera and eyes. Cut out the beak and hard spot underneath it and discard.

Rinse octopus and add to a stew pot or Dutch oven with about 3 cups water, oregano and a little vinegar; bring to a boil, covered, over medium-high heat; add salt and simmer over medium heat for 30 minutes. Liquify the ink and vinegar water in a blender along with some broth from the simmering octopus and set aside. Remove octopus and drain. When it is cool to the touch, peel off as much of the purple skin as possible and chop the meat into bite-sized pieces.

>>>>>

Pulpo continued

Meanwhile, roast the tomatoes, onion, pepper and garlic on a dry comal or in a dry cast-iron skillet over high heat. When vegetables are nicely blackened, chop and put them in a blender or food processor along with some of the cooking water from the octopus and process until well blended, or chunky if you refer.

Heat olive oil over medium heat in a skillet. Add blended vegetables and stir. Add bay leaves, cumin, salt, oregano and spices, stirring. Add reserved ink and chopped octopus to sauce and stir. Simmer about 20 minutes. Test for tenderness and add extra sour orange juice or vinegar if necessary. Serve with white rice and a sprig of fresh cilantro.

Serves 4.

Pulpo En Escabeche
Octopus in Pickled Onions

We first tasted this dish at Los Barriles, a popular seafood restaurant in Chicxulub Puerto. It has become a favorite.

2½ lbs. (1 kilo) octopus, cleaned
1 Tbl. plus ¼ cup mild vinegar
½ tsp. oregano
1 tsp. salt
2 xcatic or guero chiles
1 large white onion
2 Tbls. olive oil
½ tsp. toasted and crushed oregano
¼ tsp. EACH pepper, allspice, cumin
2 bay leaves
1 tsp. salt

If the octopus is large, peel off the purple skin under running water before cooking. Smaller octopus are easier to peel after cooking. In a stew pot or Dutch oven, cook the cleaned octopus over medium-high heat. in about 3 cups water with oregano and salt until tender, 30 to 60 minutes. Add about the tablespoon of the vinegar. When tender, remove from water and set aside to cool. When cool enough to touch, peel off any purple skin from octopus; cut the meat into bite-sized pieces.

Roast the xcatic chiles on a dry comal or in a cast-iron skillet over high heat. Slice the onion in half lengthwise and julienne in thin strips. In a large skillet, heat 1 Tbl. olive oil and saute onions over medium-high heat a few minutes, just until opaque. Remove to a plate. Add remaining olive oil. Add chopped otopus and saute along with oregano, pepper, allspice, cumin, bay leaves and salt for 2 to 3 minutes. Add onions, 1/4 cup vinegar, any accumulated juices and whole roasted chiles to octopus. Stir and simmer on low heat about 15 minutes. Serve with rice.

Serves 4

Pulpo A La Marinero

Octopus Sauteed With Tomatoes, Peppers, Onions

The caper, olives and raisins carry flavors from the Mediterranean to this Yucatecan favorite. For the white wine, we used a Chilean sauvignon-semillon blend. It worked well and also made an excellent accompaniment. Beer works well too.

2 to 3 lbs. octopus, cleaned
¼ cup mild vinegar, if needed
Olive oil
4 tomatoes, chopped
1 tsp. salt
2 cloves garlic, peeled and mashed
1 large bell pepper, julienned
1 large white onion, julienned
8 to 10 stuffed olives
10 capers
10 raisins
½ cup dry white wine
Chopped parsley or cilantro

With a wooden mallet, pound the octopus just for good measure to ensure tenderness. If it is a large octopus, you can peel off the skin before cooking. Small ones are easier to cook whole and then peel and cut up afterwards. Put the octopus in a large deep pot and cover with water. Bring to a boil over medium-high heat; turn down the heat and simmer 45 minutes. If it still feels tough, add the vinegar and continue cooking another 15 minutes.

Meanwhile, in a medium skillet over medium-high heat, saute the tomatoes in olive oil with salt and mashed garlic for a few minutes. Set aside and keep warm. When tender, remove the octopus and let it cool enough so you can peel off any of the purplish outside skin. Chop the tentacles into 1-inch rounds and slice the body and head into thin strips.

In a large skillet over medium-high heat, saute the sliced onion and pepper in olive oil. Add the olives, capers, raisins and white wine; stir to blend and simmer a few more minutes on medium heat, until raisins are plump. Add cut-up octopus and sauteed tomatoes; stir to heat through. Sprinkle with parsley or cilantro and serve with warm French bread, white rice and a simple green salad.

Serves 4.

Ensalada De Pulpo
Octopus Salad

During pulpo (octopus) season in Progreso, we are always looking for new recipes to accommodate this plentiful seasonal crop. This one, adapted from "Mexico Desconocido's Guia Gastronomica" was a big hit among friends and neighbors. Use calamari instead of octopus if you wish.

2 lbs. fresh octopus
1 tsp. salt
1 tsp. oregano
2 bay leaves
1 Tbl. vinegar
2 Roma tomatoes
1 small onion
Bunch cilantro
⅓ cup olive oil
Juice of 2 limes
2 Tbls. pulpo cooking water
Salt and pepper to taste

Clean the pulpo and cook in boiling water with salt, oregano, bay leaves and vinegar for 40 to 50 minutes, or until tender. When tender, remove and allow to cool, reserving some of the cooking water. Meanwhile, seed and chop the tomatoes, chop the onion and mince the cilantro. When the octopus is cool, peel off as much of the sticky purple skin as possible under running water. Chop the octopus into bite-sized pieces. Put chopped octopus, chopped vegetables and cilantro in a serving bowl. In a small bowl or jar combine oil, lime juice, octopus cooking water and salt and pepper to taste. Whisk or shake to blend and pour over the salad. Stir to thoroughly cover. Refrigerate for at least 1 hour before serving. If you wish, make several hours ahead and add the cilantro at the last minute, just before serving.

Serves 4 as an entree, 8 as a starter and 12 to 15 as a botana.

Tikin-Xic
Achiote-Basted Grilled Fish

Tikin-Xic has an unmistakable Mayan heritage. Although traditionally made with a whole fish, you can also use filets, individually wrapped. If you can't find banana leaves, substitute aluminum foil.

1 large grouper (5 to 6 lbs.), cleaned and butterflied
3 oz. Achiote (1 small box)
1 cup sour orange juice or half sweet orange and half mild vinegar
1 Tbl. olive oil
1 tsp. EACH salt and freshly ground pepper
2 large cloves garlic, finely chopped
3 xcatic chiles cut in strips
2 red or green bell peppers cut in strips
2 red onions cut in rings
2 Roma tomatoes cut in rounds
1 Tbl. Mexican oregano, toasted and crushed
6 to 8 oz. beer or white wine
1 large banana leaf, softened over a flame

Rinse the fish and pat dry with paper towels. Dissolve the Achiote in the juice; mix in the oil, salt and pepper. Rub the meaty side of fish with marinade, covering it thoroughly. Sprinkle chopped garlic on top and let fish marinate 30 minutes to 1 hour. Place fish, skin side down on top of the banana leaf with enough overlap so it can be wrapped. Sprinkle the chiles, peppers, onion rings and tomato slices on top of the fish. Sprinkle toasted oregano on top of the vegetables. Pour the beer (or wine) on top and wrap. Cook on a grill over hot coals for about 30 minutes, or on a baking sheet in a 350-degree oven for 45 minutes, leaving the wrapper open for the final 10 minutes to let the vegetables brown a little. Serve with rice or roasted potatoes, a simple salad and tortillas if you wish.

Serves 8.

Tamales, Panuchos, Salbutes

Historians estimate that the Maya began to process corn or *maize* into dough around 1000 B.C. They soaked the kernels in lime (calcium carbonate) or wood ash so they would be easier to grind. But more importantly, this process releases essential nutrients and enhances the protein value of the resulting dough or *masa*. Without this essential soaking, scholars speculate the Maya would have not have developed beyond the village level into a highly evolved culture of pyramid- builders, astronomers and mathematicians.

Many Maya today still hold corn in high regard. Not only is it the "staff of life," but the soul of life, because man was made from corn – rather than mud – according to the Mayan myth of creation. The corn god, Yum Kaax, ranks high among Mayan deities and is still venerated by some indigenous people.

Corn masa is used to make a variety of foods including tortillas and "atole," a breakfast beverage, but many believe the *creme de la creme* of all masa-based dishes is the tamale. Although made throughout Mexico, tamales reach their culinary pinnacle in the Yucatan, where an array of techniques are used to season, fill, assemble and cook them. Whether rolled like a jellyroll cake or layered like lasagna, they are wrapped in banana leaves, and then either steamed on top of the stove or baked in an oven or underground pit called a "pib".

Colados, a type of tamale unique to the Yucatan, have a tender texture that is achieved by precooking and straining the masa to make it silky smooth.

Also unique to the Yucatan are brazos. Dating back to pre-conquest days, brazos are tamales made with chaya, a spinach-type leaf, and filled with a mixture of hard-cooked eggs and ground pumpkin seeds.

Panuchos, another corn-based regional specialty, are hand-made tortillas that are stuffed with refried black beans and topped with shredded chicken and pickled red onions. Salbutes are deep-fried tortillas with shredded meat or chicken and various garnishes, including avocado or cucumber and lettuce.

Codzitos
Rolled and Fried Tacos

You might recognize this dish by the name Taquitos. Here in the Yucatan, they are called Codzitos and they can be filled with leftover shredded or ground meat or simply rolled tight and topped with tomato sauce and grated cheese. They make a great appetizer.

1 cup cooked, shredded or ground meat or poultry
24 corn tortillas
24 toothpicks
Oil
1 cup fresh tomato sauce
Shredded lettuce
1 cup grated cheese (Manchego, Monterrey Jack)
Cilantro

Heat the meat and sprinkle a spoonful down the center of each tortilla. Roll them up and fasten each with a toothpick. Heat about 2 tablespoons of oil on medium-high heat in a large, heavy-bottomed non-stick skillet. Brown the rolled tacos, 8 at a time. Spoon hot oil over the tops of the rolled tacos to make them brown evenly. Add more oil as needed (or use a deep fry). Meanwhile, heat the tomato sauce on medium heat just until it starts to boil; lower and simmer about 3 or 4 minutes, just to heat through. When the rolled tacos are browned, drain on paper towels. Put a bed of shredded lettuce on each plate. Place 4 rolled tacos on top and finish with tomato sauce. Garnish with grated cheese and cilantro. Sprinkle extra lettuce on top if you wish.

Serves 6.

Tamales Colados
Pre-cooked Tamales

Also known as Tamales de Cuchara or Tamales de Boda, these tamales are so tender they can be eaten with a spoon (cuchara). What makes them tender is pre-cooking and straining the masa. Years ago it was the custom to serve these tamales at wedding breakfasts, following a nuptial Mass, thus the name Tamales de Boda. In this recipe we take a short cut by using masa flour, so the dough does not have to be strained. If you use prepared masa, you must strain the dough before assembling.

 4 lbs. chicken, cut up
2 Tbls. Achiote
1 tsp. oregano
½ tsp. cumin
2 large cloves garlic, mashed
½ stem epazote
Salt and black pepper to taste
2 tsp. chicken bouillon
½ white onion, chopped
3 tomatoes, coarsely chopped
1 bell pepper, seeded and chopped
1 tsp. oil
2 cups reserved achiote-flavored chicken broth
½ cup masa or wheat flour
¼ white onion, finely chopped
1 cup melted lard
4 cups masa harina (flour)
2 cups water
1 stem epazote
1 tsp. salt
1 package banana leaves

Bring 2 qts. water to boil on high heat. In a small bowl, dissolve Achiote in ½ cup water. Strain into the pot. Add chicken, oregano, cumin, mashed garlic, epazote, salt, pepper and bouillon. Lower heat and simmer about 30 minutes; remove chicken and reserve broth. When cool enough to handle, shred chicken into tiny pieces.

>>>>>

Tamales Colados continued

In a frying pan, saute onion, tomato and pepper in oil on medium-high heat. Add 2 cups reserved achiote-flavored chicken broth; dissolve flour in some broth and add to pan; simmer on low heat until it thickens like a gravy; add salt to taste.

In a large pot or Dutch oven on medium heat, saute the finely chopped onion in a little of the melted lard. In a large bowl, gradually blend the masa flour and water. Add salt and more water as needed to form a thin batter; add mixture to the simmering onions along with epazote and stir. Continue stirring, adding lard gradually, as you would add broth to risotto, until it thickens, 10 to 15 minutes. When the mixture holds its shape, pour onto a large platter or baking pan to cool.

Assembly: Wipe banana leaves clean with a damp cloth before using. Cut or tear into rectangles, approximately 9-by-7 inches. Save extra pieces to use for patches in case any leaves tear during wrapping. Tear off the center ribs of the leaves and divide into thin ribbons for tying. Spread rectangles on a clean counter top or table. Ladle about 2 Tbls. of masa into the center of each leaf, make a well in the center. Put several pieces of chicken in each well. Top with Salsa de Achiote, including some tomato, onion and pepper in each tamale.

To wrap, fold one of the longer sides of the leaf up and over the filling and press down lightly to seal masa around filling. Repeat with the other side and fold the ends up to form a neat package. Tie with fiber ribbons around all four sides. Place in a steamer or tamale cooker. If you don't have a steamer, put an oven-proof saucer upside down in the bottom of a pot and place an oven rack on top. Bring 2 to 3 cups water (depending on size of steamer) to boil. Carefully place tamales on rack over the boiling water. Steam for 1 hour. When removing tamales from the steamer, use a spatula, because the ribbon may break or slip, dumping the tamale out into the pot. Serve with Salsa de Tomate or a red salsa if you prefer. (Tamales can be frozen after cooling.)

Makes 20 tamales.

Vaporcitos
Chicken Tamales

Vaporcitos, from "vapor" or steam, is another name for tamales in the Yucatan. These chicken tamales are also known as Tamales de Ticul, after the town of Ticul about 50 miles from Merida. In the evening on street corners throughout the region, in cities and pueblos alike, venders sell hot, home-cooked vaporcitos from a big steamer for 60 to 70 cents each.

4 lbs. chicken, cut up
2 Tbls. achiote paste
1 tsp. oregano
½ tsp EACH cumin, freshly ground black pepper
2 large cloves garlic, mashed
½ stem epazote
2 tsp. chicken bouillon
Kol (Sauce):
½ white onion, chopped
3 tomatoes, coarsely chopped
½ green bell pepper or a few serrano chiles, seeded, deveined and chopped
½ cup masa harina
Masa:
4 cups masa harina (flour) or 2¼ lbs. fresh masa
2 to 2½ cups water
1 to 1½ cup melted lard
1 tsp. salt
1 package banana leaves

Bring 2 qts. water to boil in a stew pot or Dutch oven on high heat. In a bowl, dilute achiote paste in ½ cup water by rubbing to dissolve the paste with your fingers or a fork. Strain into the pot. Cut the chicken into pieces, rinse, remove skin if desired; add chicken parts to boiling water. Stir in oregano, cumin, mashed garlic, epazote, pepper, salt and bouillon. When chicken is cooked, about 30 to 40 minutes, remove from pot and cool on a plate. Reserve broth.

>>>>

Vaporcitos continued

For the Kol (Sauce): In a frying pan, saute onion, tomatoes and pepper in a little lard for a few minutes on medium-high heat. Add 1 cup reserved chicken broth. Dissolve masa harina in a cup of broth and add to the simmering mixture. Stir to thicken. Add salt or bouillon to taste and extra broth if needed; set aside.

For the Masa: In a large bowl, gradually blend the masa flour and water. Continue stirring, add salt and gradually mix in the lard until mixture holds its shape and glistens when you put some in your hand. Let the masa rest while you prepare banana leaves. (If you use fresh masa, you will need less water and lard.)

Assembly: Wipe banana leaves with a clean, damp cloth. Cut or tear into rectangles, approximately 9-by-7 inches. Save extra pieces to use for patches in case any leaves tear during wrapping. Tear off the center ribs of the leaves and divide into thin ribbons for tying. Spread rectangles on a counter top or table. Form masa into balls, slightly larger than golf balls and put one in the center of each leaf. Using your fingers, pat dough into a tortilla. Put several pieces of shredded chicken and a good dollop of Kol in the center of each. Fold one of the longer sides of the banana leaf up over the filling. Pull the leaf back leaving the masa folded over. Fold up the opposite side and leave the leaf there. Bring the original side up and fold over the top. Fold up the short ends to form a neat package and tie with fiber ribbons around all four sides.

Place in a steamer with 2 to 3 cups (depending on size of steamer) boiling water. You will probably need to improvise two steamers to cook 20 tamales. If you don't have a steamer, put an oven-proof plate upside down in the bottom of a large pot. Carefully place tamales on inverted plate. Steam for 1 hour. When removing tamales from the steamer, use a spatula, because the ties may break or slip and dump the tamale out of their wrapers into the pot. Tamales can be frozen after cooling. Serve with tomato sauce or a spicy salsa if you wish.

Makes 20 tamale

Tamalitos de Espelon
Fresh Bean Tamales With Chicken and Pork Filling

Espelon are fresh beans similar in appearance to black-eyed peas. Yucatecans traditionally eat these tamales for the Mayan feast of Hanal Pixan or the Catholics' All Saints and All Souls Day. But they can be made and eaten anytime the fresh beans are available. Since black-eyed peas are traditionally eaten for good luck around the New Year in the U.S., anytime in December or January would be appropriate for a feast of Tamalitos de Espelon.

1 whole chicken breast, cut up
1 lb. pork loin or shoulder cut in chunks
1 clove garlic
1 tsp. salt
½ tsp. cumin
1 tsp. crushed oregano
½ tsp. black pepper
1 stalk epazote, if available
1 cup fresh espelon or fresh black-eyed peas
1 kg. fresh masa, or about 4 cups masa harina (flour)
½ lb. fresh lard
2 tsp. salt
1 tsp. oil
½ medium white onion, minced
¼ bell pepper, minced
2 small tomatoes, minced
1 clove garlic, minced
1½ Tbls. Achiote
1 tsp. chicken bouillon
1½ cups broth from pork and chicken
1 pkg. banana leaves
2 cups Tomato Sauce

>>>>>

Tamalitos de Espelon continued

Put the chicken and pork in a large pot with enough water to cover and bring to a boil on high heat. Add garlic, salt, cumin, oregano and pepper. Cover and simmer on low heat for 30 to 40 minutes. When the meat is cooked through, set aside to cool, reserving broth. Rinse the beans and cook in boiling water with the epazote until tender, 15 to 30 minutes depending on their age. Do not overcook.

If you use masa flour, prepare according to package directions and set aside. With fresh masa, put it in a bowl or pan with a flat bottom and spread it out as much as possible. Pour a little boiling water on top of it and punch holes in the masa with your fingers to let the water seep in. Now fold the masa over itself as you would with a bread dough to incorporate the water. Meanwhile, Drain the beans and add them to the prepared masa along with the lard and 2 tsp. salt. Work the beans and lard into the masa with your hands until you have a soft, pliable dough. Let it rest.

In a medium saucepan, heat the oil over medium heat; add the onion, bell pepper, tomatoes and garlic, stirring to saute. Dissolve the Achiote with some reserved broth and add to the pan along with remaining broth and chicken bouillon. Stir and simmer over low heat. When meat is cool enough to touch, shred and add to mixture, stirring to blend well.

Assembly: Clean off a counter or tabletop. Wipe banana leaves clean. Remove center spines and discard. Cut or tear leaves into 7-by-9-inch pieces. Save small pieces to patch torn leaves. Put about a third cup masa in the center of a prepared leaf and pat out into a thin disk like a tortilla, leaving 1½ to 2 inches at the ends for folding. Put a tablespoon or so of filling in the center of each. To wrap, bring one of the long sides up over the filling and pat the masa down over it, pulling the leaf back. Now fold the opposite side up over the filling, pat it down and fold over the first side again. Fold up the short ends. These little tamales do not have to be tied as they are small and fairly firm. Put them on a steamer rack in a large pot with 2 to 3 inches boiling water, cover and steam on medium heat for about 1 hour. (If you don't have a steamer rack, put a heat-resistant plate in the bottom of a Dutch oven or stew pot to make a shelf and put the tamales on top of it.) Serve with tomato sauce.

Makes about 24

Tamales de Chaya

Chaya Wrapped Tamales With Ground Meat Filling

A variation on Brazos de Reina and Dzotobichay, this tamale from Campeche is filled with a seasoned ground meat mixture called Picadillo. Although pork is the traditional filling, you can use beef or a mixture of both. These can be served as an appetizer or entree, depending on their size and quantity.

40 to 50 large chaya leaves, Swiss chard or spinach, about 1 lb.
4 cups (1 lb.) masa flour
4 oz. liquified lard or 3 oz. oil
½ tsp. salt
1 pkg. banana leaves

Picadillo:
Oil
1 clove garlic, mashed
1 lb. ground pork, beef or a mixture of both
¼ white onion, finely chopped
1 tomato chopped
¼ tsp. cumin
1 tsp. oregano
1 tsp. each pepper, salt
1 Tbls. each raisins, capers, olives, coarsely chopped
1 egg, beaten with 1 Tbl. water
1 Tbls. flour

Garnish:
Fresh tomato sauce
¼ cup toasted and ground pumpkin seeds (pepita molida)
1 large hard-cooked egg

>>>>>

Tamales de Chaya continued

Rinse the chaya, chard or spinach. Cut into strips, chiffonard style. In a large pot, put water to boil on medium-high heat; add chaya and parboil 2 to 3 minutes. Drain, reserving some water. In a medium-sized bowl, combine masa flour with 2 or 3 tablespoons of chaya cooking water and mix with a fork or wooden spoon. If using lard, heat to liquid and add to mix. Add salt and more liquid as needed to form a smooth dough. Add the parboiled chaya; blend well and let it rest.

For the Picadillo: In a medium-sized skillet, saute garlic in oil on medium-high heat. Add ground meat, onion and continue sauteing. Add tomato, cumin, oregano, pepper and salt, stirring and sauteing until meat is no longer pink. Remove from heat. When cool enough to handle, add egg and flour and blend well.

Assembly: If banana leaves are fresh, pass each side over a flame or high heat briefly to make them soft and pliable. Wipe clean and cut into 20 rectangles, 9-by-7 inches. Save the fibrous center stems and shred them for ties. Put a large serving spoon of masa on each leaf and spread it out a bit; top with 2 Tbls. picadillo. Bring one long side of banana leaf up and use it to fold the masa over on itself; now fold the leaves over each other; fold up the short ends and tie with fibrous strips. In a covered steamer or large pot fitted with a plate or rack to keep tamales above the water, heat about 2 inches of water to boiling; lower heat and steam tamales 45 minutes.

Garnish: Remove tamales from banana leaves. Overlap them on a large platter. Pour some tomato sauce in a band down the middle, and sprinkle ground pumpkin seeds and chopped egg on top. Pass remaining tomato sauce in a bowl or small pitcher.

Makes 20 tamales.

Brazo de Reina

Chaya, Egg and Ground Pumpkin Seed Tamale

A brazo is a long, thick tamale that resembles a "brazo" or arm. Some people call this dish Brazo de Indio and attribute the "Reina" (queen) nomenclature to another version with ground meat filling, like Tamales de Chaya, but larger. (Not to confuse the issue, there is also a jellyroll cake covered with meringue that is known as a Brazo de Reina.)

9 large eggs
1 bunch chaya leaves (spinach or Swiss chard), about ½ lb.
2 cups masa flour or 1 lb. prepared masa (dough)
2 Tbls. flour
3 oz. (100 g.) lard or oil
½ tsp. salt
6 Tbls. toasted and ground pumpkin seeds (pepita molida)
1 pkg. banana leaves or aluminum foil
Fresh Tomato Sauce

In a large sauce pan, cover eggs with water and bring to boil on high heat; lower heat and simmer for 15 minutes. Wearing rubber gloves to protect your hands, rinse the chaya, pull off the stems; cut the leaves into strips, like a chiffonard, and parboil in about 2 cups of water on high heat for about five minutes, stirring occasionally. Drain, reserving some water to make the masa (dough).

In a medium-sized bowl, combine masa harina or prepared masa with a tablespoon of chaya cooking water and mix with a fork or wooden spoon. Add oil or lard — melt lard in a microwave or small skillet on low heat. Add salt, flour and more chaya water if necessary to form a smooth dough. Mix in the chopped chaya leaves and blend well.

> > > > >

Brazo de Reina *continued*

If fresh, pass banana leaves over a flame or high heat to soften for easier handling. Wipe leaves with a clean cloth. Cut into six 10-inch-by-14-inch rectangles, two for each brazo. Save the fibrous center ribs for ties.

Spread one-third of the masa and chaya mixture to within a ½ inch of the edge of one rectangle. Peel the eggs and slice off their pointy ends. Mince the cut off ends and reserve for garnish. Sprinkle 2 Tbls. ground pumpkin seeds down the center of the brazo and lay three eggs end to end on top of the ground seeds. Bring the longer sides of banana leaf together, forming the masa into a log. Fold up the ends, wrap another leaf around the log and tie with fibrous strips. Repeat for two more brazos.

Put the three brazos in a large covered steamer with 2 to 3 inches of water in the bottom, or use a large pot fitted with a rack or inverted plate to hold the wrapped brazos above the water. Bring water to a boil and steam the brazos over medium heat for 45 minutes. Carefully remove brazos from steamer, take off the banana-leaf wrappers and slice brazos into ¾-inch thick rounds. Serve with warm tomato sauce and a garnish of chopped egg whites.

Serves 6 to 8.

Mucbilpollo
Chicken and Pork Tamale Pie

Day of the Dead, or "Hanal Pixan" in Maya, is celebrated in the Yucatan with this traditional dish. The forerunner of Tamale Pie, it has a top and bottom layer of masa enclosing a filling of seasoned pork and chicken. Wrapped in banana leaves and baked (either underground in a "pib" or in a conventional oven), Mucbipollo is prepared as a ritual offering for the dead, and it is eaten at family gatherings at this time of year. A cup of hot chocolate is the traditional beverage, but red wine is good too.

Filling:
1 qt. chicken broth or water and bouillon
½ small head garlic, roasted
½ small white onion, roasted
1 small chicken, cut up, or 2¼ lbs. chicken breasts
1 lb. pork leg, loin or shoulder, cut up
¼ tsp. EACH cumin, black pepper, freshly ground allspice
½ tsp. EACH salt, oregano
2 stems epazote, if available
½ white onion, chopped
4 Roma tomatoes, chopped
1 bell pepper, seeded and chopped
1 Serrano chile, seeded, deveined and chopped
Salt to taste
Lard or oil
1½ oz. Achiote
½ cup flour
2 Tbls. fresh masa

Masa:
1 lb. fresh masa
¼ lb. lard, melted, or oil
2 tsp. salt
1 pkg. banana leaves

>>>>>

Mucbilpollo continued

Filling: Put broth or water and bouillon to boil on high heat in a Dutch oven. Meanwhile, char the onion and garlic on a hot comal. Cut up chicken and pork and rinse before adding to pot. Add cumin, pepper, allspice, salt, oregano, epazote; return to a boil, reduce heat and simmer. Add roasted onion and garlic, cover and cook about 30 minutes. When tender, remove meat and set aside; reserve broth. When cool enough to handle, separate chicken and pork into bite-sized pieces and set aside. Discard skin and bones. Make a sauce by heating about 2 Tbls. lard in a frypan. Add onion, tomato, pepper and chile and saute on medium-high heat until tender. Remove and set aside. Dissolve Achiote in a ½ cup of simmering chicken broth and strain into lard in frypan. Lower heat to medium. Add ½ cup flour and stir. Dissolve 2 Tbls. masa in some broth and strain into pan; continue stirring and adding broth as needed. Taste and adjust seasonings if necessary. Strain back any liquid that has accumulated around the sauteed vegetables and continue stirring sauce until smooth and thick, about 15 minutes.

Masa: Gradually add melted lard to masa and blend by hand. Add salt and continue to work the dough into a smooth texture that holds together well. Smear a little dough on a banana leaf. If it leaves a film of grease, it is ready. If not, add more lard.

Assembly: Line a 9-inch-by-14-inch baking pan (or two 8- or 9-inch cake or pie tins) with banana leaves large enough to drap over the edges of the pan. Press 2/3 of the dough into the bottom and up the sides of the pan. Put chicken and pork pieces on top. Add sauteed vegetables evenly over chicken and top with the masa-thickened sauce, saving about a ½ cup for the top. Bring the top edges of masa down over the filling by pulling the banana leaves toward the center and peeling the masa away from the leaves. Flatten remaining masa on two overlapping banana leaves and press out into a rectangle the size of the baking pan. Carefully lift the masa-covered leaves and turn over on top of the filling. Peel away the leaves; seal the edges of the masa and spread the rest of the sauce on top. Cover with banana leaves and bake on lower rack of oven at 400 degrees for 45 minutes. Remove top leaves and continue cooking until top is browned, about 15 minutes more.

Serves 6 to 8.

Mini Mucbilpollo
Achiote-Seasoned Chicken Croquettes

In Merida around the main plaza, street venders sell Mini Mucbilpollos. We served them at a going-away party for our "snowbird" visitors one year and they were the hit of the evening. Guests couldn't wait for the next serving, sizzling hot from the skillet.

Filling:
1 qt. chicken broth or water and chicken bouillon
½ small head garlic, roasted
½ small white onion, roasted
2¼ lbs. (1 kg.) chicken breasts
¼ tsp. EACH cumin, freshly ground black pepper
⅛ tsp. freshly ground allspice
½ tsp. EACH salt, oregano
½ white onion, chopped
4 Roma tomatoes, chopped
1 bell pepper, seeded and chopped
1 Serrano chile, seeded, deveined and chopped
Salt to taste
Lard or oil
1 ½ oz. Achiote
½ cup flour
2 Tbls. masa

Masa:
1 lb. fresh masa, or equivalent masa harina
¼ lb. lard, melted, or oil
2 tsp. salt

>>>>>

Mini Mucbilpollo continued

Filling: Put broth or water and bouillon on to boil in a Dutch oven on medium-high heat. Meanwhile, on a hot comal, char-broil the onion and garlic. Cut up chicken and rinse before adding to pot. Add cumin, pepper, allspice, salt and oregano; bring to boil and reduce heat to simmer. Add roasted onion and garlic, cover and cook about 20 minutes more. When tender, remove meat and set aside; reserve broth. When cool enough to handle, separate chicken into bite-sized pieces. Discard skin and bones. Heat about 2 Tbls. lard in a skillet on medium-high heat. Add onion, tomato, pepper and chile and saute until tender. Dissolve Achiote in a ½ cup of reserved chicken broth and strain into skillet. Add ½ cup flour and stir. Dissolve 2 Tbls. masa in some broth and strain into pan; continue stirring and adding broth as needed until smooth and thick, about 15 minutes. Add shredded chicken to sauce; taste and adjust seasonings if necessary.

Masa: Gradually add melted lard to masa and blend by hand. Add salt and continue to work the dough into a smooth texture that holds together well. Smear a little dough on a clean counter top; if it leaves a film of grease it is ready. If not, add more lard.

Assembly: On a piece of plastic wrap press a 2 inch chunk of masa out into a thick round and put a dollop of the chicken and sauce in the middle. Fold the sides over and form into an egg or oval shape. Meanwhile, in a large, heavy skillet, heat about ½ inch lard or oil to very hot and brown the ovals or patties, five or six at a time, depending on pan size. Spoon hot oil over the top of each Mini Mucbilpollo to hasten browning. Drain on paper towels and serve immediately on a lettuce-lined platter.

Makes about 30.

Panuchos
Stuffed Open-face Tacos

Panuchos are synonymous with the Yucatan. They begin with handmade corn tortillas that are heated on a comal until they puff up, whereupon an opening is made in the puffed layer so it can be filled with refried black beans. This is not easy to do, but fun to try. Throughout the Yucatan, you can buyfresh or frozen pre-stuffed panuchos. (Or take a shortcut, as we do, and spread the beans on top of a lightly fried tortilla before you add the toppings.) Leftover Pollo Pibil goes great in this dish.

½ turkey breast or whole chicken breast
1 Tbl. Achiote paste (or use liquid achiote)
1 large banana leaf
24 fresh corn tortillas, lightly crisped in oil
1 cup refried black beans
Cebolla Encurtida (Pickled Red Onions)
2 avocados, peeled and thinly sliced
Shredded lettuce
1 cucumber, peeled, seeded and sliced

In a large bowl, dissolve the Achiote in a little sour orange juice or vinegar (or use liquid Achiote) with a pinch of salt. Add the turkey or chicken breast and marinate for about 15 minutes. Bake the turkey or chicken breast in a 350-degree oven wrapped in a banana leaf, or foil, for about 30 minutes. Open the wrapper and continue baking for 15 to 20 minutes more, until fully cooked. Set aside and let it cool before shredding it by hand.

Assembly: Heat the tortillas on a comal, spread with refried beans and top with shredded turkey or chicken, pickled red onions, sliced avocado, sliced cucumber and shredded lettuce.

Makes 24 Panucho.

Dzotobichay
Chaya Wrapped Tamales

The chaya leaves are left whole and wrapped around the masa in this recipe. In other versions the chaya is chopped and added to the masa, as in Brazos de Reina. In yet another variation, the eggs are left whole the ground pumpkin seeds are sprinkled on top of the tamale as a garnish. However you make them, you will be experiencing a bit of culinary history when you bite into these hearty tamales of Mayan heritage.

½ lb. large-leaf chaya, spinach or chard, cleaned and stemmed
1 cup green pumpkin seeds
4 hard-cooked eggs, peeled and chopped
1 lb. fresh corn masa
¼ lb. lard, melted
½ tsp. salt
Kitchen string
Fresh Tomato Sauce

Put about an inch of water in the bottom of a steamer or large pot fitted with a vegetable steamer and bring water to boil on medium-high heat. When the water begins to steam, add the chaya leaves, a few at a time and steam a few minutes, until tender. Remove and allow to dry on a clean counter or tray. Meanwhile, toast the pumpkin seeds in a dry skillet over medium heat until golden. Remove from heat. When cool, grind seeds in a spice mill or food processor to the texture of fine breadcrumbs.

Place masa in a mixing bowl and gradually add a few drops of water, salt and melted lard, working it with your fingers to form a smooth dough. (If you prefer, you can use masa harina — Maseca brand is best — instead of prepared dough, and follow package instruction. Let dough rest a few minutes.

Divide masa into 8 pieces; roll each into a ball and pat out on two overlapping chaya leaves. Sprinkle with ground pumpkin seeds and chopped egg, evenly divided. Fold one side over the other and fold or tuck in the short ends. Tie with string, and steam on low heat for about 45 minutes. Serve with fresh tomato sauce.

Makes 8 tamales.

Polkanes
Bean and Pumpkin-Seed Patties

These little appetizers used to be formed into in the shape of a snake's head, which is what "polkane" means in Maya, but today many people just pat them into little rounds. A seasonal dish, they are made in November when ibes (similar to butter beans or baby limas), are available. Compared to dry beans, fresh ibes are expensive, so Polkanes are quite a treat. Like many dishes with ancient Mayan roots, Polkanes are meatless.

¾ to 1 lb. fresh ibes (butter beans or fresh baby limas)
1 stem epazote, if available
1 tsp. salt
½ cup toasted and ground pepitas (pumpkin seeds)
1 bunch cebollina (chives or green onions)
½ bunch cilantro
Juice of 1 sour orange or some leftover bean liquid
2¼ lbs.(1 kg.) masa
1½ tsp. salt
½ cup water
3 Tbls. flour
Oil
Salsa Xni-Pec

Put the beans in a medium saucepan with enough water to cover and bring to a boil on high heat. Add epazote and salt, cover and simmer on low for 15 minutes, or until tender. Do not overcook. Drain the beans and reserve a little cooking water. Add the ground pepitas to the beans. While the beans cool, mince the chives and leaves of cilantro and add to the bean mixture. Toss and add salt and pepper to taste. Meanwhile, prepare the masa by adding salt and flour and then water, a little at a time. Work it with your hands into a smooth dough. Set aside to rest about 15 minutes.

Assembly: Divide masa into 24 1½-inch balls. Pat each ball out into a small tortilla in the palm of your hand. Put in a tablespoon of bean filling and work the masa up around the filling. Pat into a flat disc. Fry the Polkanes in ¼ inch of hot oil on medium-high heat and drain on paper towels. Serve with Xni-Pec.

Makes 24.

Salbutes
Tostadas With Seasoned Meat Topping

These little tacos or tostadas rank right next to panuchos as the favored snack or "merienda" served in the open-air cafes that line Merida's Paseo de Montejo, a street fashioned after Paris' Champs Elysees.   Salbutes vary from Panuchos in that they are not stuffed with refried beans. Toppings can be very similar.

Oil
24 small corn tortillas
2 Roma tomatoes, chopped
1 large clove garlic, mashed
¼ large white onion, chopped
¼ bell pepper, chopped
1 lb. ground pork or a mixture of pork and beef, or shredded chicken
½ tsp. crushed oregano
¼ tsp. EACH, cumin, freshly ground black pepper
Salt to taste
<u>**Toppings:**</u>
6 or 8 lettuce leaves, shredded or torn into taco size bits
1 large tomato, thinly sliced
2 or 3 avocados or a cucumber, peeled and sliced
Pickled Red Onions (Cebolla Encurtida)
Habanero salsa, if desired

In a large skillet heat about ¼ inch oil on medium-high heat and try the tortillas until crisp. Drain on paper towels. Prepare the vegetables and saute them in oil on medium heat until they start to go limp. Add the ground meat (or chicken) and seasonings and continue to saute. Cook until all of the liquid evaporates and the meat is no longer pink, about 15 minutes.

Assemby: Top each tortilla with a piece of lettuce, a tablespoon ground meat mixture, a slice of tomato, avocado or cucumber and a sprinkling of pickled onion. If you wish, serve some habanero salsa on the side.

Makes 24 salbutes.

Tamalitos de Puerco Arrollados
Tamales With Seasoned Pork Filling

Another name for these little tamales is "serpentinos" because they are rolled up like a snake and tied at either end. Of course, you can make them the traditional way as well and just fold the ends over. We made them one Christmas Eve, along with chicken tamales. The "serpentinos" with their savory filling proved to be the favorite.

2¼ lbs. (1 kilo) pork leg or loin, ground
1 Tbl. Achiote
1 Tbl. Recado Bistec
½ tsp. EACH salt, allspice
2 or 3 cloves garlic, roasted, peeled and mashed
1 lb. tomatoes
4 to 6 stems of epazote
1 or 2 habanero chiles, if desired
3 lbs. masa
Salt
½ lb. lard
1 pkg. banana leaves

Trim as much fat from the pork as possible and grind it roughly, or have it trimmed and ground by the butcher. In a large bowl, put a heaping tablespoon of Achiote paste, or 2 Tbls. Liquid Achiote, along with the Recado Bistec, salt, allspice and mashed, roasted garlic. Add a quarter to half cup water to dissolve the recados and make a marinade. Add the pork and stir to incorporate to cover all of the pork with the marinade.. Chop the tomatoes and seed them over a strainer to catch the juices. Add the chopped tomatoes and their juice to the mixture and stir.

In a large, deep skillet heat a bit of the lard over medium heat and add the ground pork mixture. When the mixture begins to boil, check it for seasoning and add more salt if necessary. Stir gently to keep it from sticking. Add one or two whole habaneros to the mix, if you wish, and stir. Don't let the habanero break open. When the mixture is almost dry, take a small chunk of masa, about the size of a small tangerine, dissolve it in ½ cup of water and add it to the pan to thicken the filling. (You can use flour if you wish.) Stir to incorporate

>>>>>

Tamalitos Arrollados continued

and let it simmer on low until it thickens. Remove from the heat and let it cool while you prepare the masa. Taste the filling and remove the habaneros if it is getting too hot.

Put the rest of the masa in a large, shallow bowl or pan with a flat bottom and spread it out as much as possible. Pour a little boiling water on top of it and punch holes in the masa with your fingers to let the water seep in. Now fold the masa over itself as you would with a bread dough to incorporate the water. Add a scant teaspoon of salt. Taste and add more salt if you wish. Heat the lard until it is liquid and add a quarter cup or so to the masa, incorporating it by hand. Keep adding liquid lard until the masa feels smooth. Test the masa by smearing a little on a piece of banana leaf. If it leaves a shiny grease mark on the leaf, it is ready. Another test is that it no longer sticks to your hands.

With a clean cloth or paper towel, wipe the banana leaves on both sides. Tear the leaves in half along the center rib and divide the ribs into thin strips to use for ties. Tear or cut the leaves into rectangles about 7-by-9 inches. With the shinier side of the leaf up, put a piece of masa along the edge where the center rib was and pat it out with your fingers, as you would to make a tortilla, into a thin oblong large enough to hold a filling. Leave enough on the ends for tying. Now add a good amount of pork filling, along the length of the masa, like a sausage. Pick up the leaf along the filled edge and double it over so the masa covers the filling. You may need to press the edges of the masa together with your fingers. Now roll it up like a sausage and tie the ends, like a party favor. If the middle needs securing, put another tie on it but do not tie it tight. Continue until you run out of masa, leaves or filling.

Put two to three inches of water in a steamer and bring the water to boil. Layer the tamales in the steamer basket, putting each layer in opposite directions to prevent them from sticking together and to aid even steaming. Cover and steam for at least 1 hour. Check to make sure you don't run out of water. Test the masa after 1 hour. If it is nice and spongy, it is ready. Serve with a fresh tomato sauce if you wish.

Makes about 30 to 40.

Vegetables & Casseroles

Mayan cooking, which is at the heart of the region's cuisine, is essentially plant-based, depending on corn and beans for most of its nutrients. Post conquest cuisine is also heavily dependent on vegetables. Tomatoes, onions, garlic and bell peppers (or chile dulce) are starters for main dishes, soups and sauces of all kinds. Two types of squash are common as well: the Yucatecan squash, which is like a pattypan, and the pear-shaped chayote.

In her book, America's First Cuisines, food historian Sophie Coe says the Maya ate a variety of greens that grew in the wild. The one that has endured and is still eaten today, both for its flavor and nutritional value, is chaya, a leafy green similar to spinach and Swiss chard. A member of the Euphorbia family, chaya leaves can be irritating to the hands. The best advice is to use gloves when washing the leaves or to plunge the leaves into hot water several times before handling.

A government study published in 1974 established what the indigenous people knew instinctively: Chaya is rich in protein, more nutritious than spinach, and superior to corn in all but phosphorous and carbohydrate. According to the study, 3½ ounces of chaya have the following: Protein 9%, fat 2%, carbohydrate 7%. In addition, it has 421 mg. calcium, 63 mg. phosphorous, 11 mg. iron. High in vitamin C, it has 274 mg., plus 8 mg. vitamin A, 1.7 mg. niacin, and small quantities of vitamins B1 and B2.

Although potatoes and other vegetables, such as eggplant, figure prominently in the region's cooking, they are usually incorporated into main dishes, as in Chancletas de Berenjena (eggplant), or appear in appetizers such as Botana de Papas, instead of being served on the side.

Botana de Papas

Potato Appetizer

In the state of Yucatan, law requires that food be served with drinks. This has led to the development of a specific type of restaurant that specializes in botanas or little tapas-like dishes that are served free of charge when you order a drink. Here is one of those dishes.

1 or 2 large cooked potatoes
¼ to ½ white onion
Lime juice
Salt, pepper, oregano
1 habanero, serrano or jalapeno chile

Cut cooked potatoes into ½ inch cubes; slice the onion; sprinkle with lime juice, salt, pepper and oregano. Roast, seed and devein the chile and mix it in with the potatoes. Serve as an appetizer with corn chips or tostaditas. (For a shortcut, mix the cubed potatoes with a small can of pickled jalapeno peppers en escabeche.)

Makes about 1 cup, depending on size of potatoes.

Cacerola de Chaya
Chaya Souffle

This attractive and delicious side dish can be used for a brunch entree as is, or in a pie crust for a quiche. You can double the ingredients easily.

3 cups of chaya (substitute spinach or Swiss chard)
¼ medium white onion, chopped
Oil
4 eggs, lightly beaten
1 cup milk
½ tsp. salt
¼ tsp. EACH freshly ground nutmeg and black pepper
¼ cup EACH bread crumbs and Parmesan or similar dry cheese
Butter

Rinse the chaya and chop it into thin strips. In a skillet on medium-high heat saute the chopped onion in a little oil or butter for a few minutes. Add the chopped chaya and saute until it is limp. Mix the chaya and sauteed onion with the eggs, milk, salt, nutmeg and pepper. Butter a 7-inch-by-4-inch loaf pan and pour in the chaya mixture. Sprinkle on the bread crumbs and grated cheese and bake for 15 minutes in a 425-degree oven.

Serves 4.

Chancletas de Chayote
Stuffed Chayote Squash

Chancletas means slippers or sandals which describes the slipper-shaped appearance of the chayote squash used in this dish, which is also made with eggplant.

4 medium chayotes (or 2 medium eggplants)
1 Tbl. corn oil
1 small or ½ large white onion, finely chopped
½ small bell pepper, finely chopped
1 large clove garlic, mashed
1 lb. ground pork or pork and beef mixed
½ tsp. EACH salt, freshly ground black pepper, oregano
1 tsp. EACH chopped capers, chopped olives
½ cup or more breadcrumbs
Butter
Tomato Sauce, optional

Put a pot with about a quart of water to boil over high heat. Rinse and cut the chayotes in half lengthwise; add to pot, cover and simmer until tender when pierced with a fork, about 30 minutes. (Eggplant will cook faster.) Remove and set aside.

In a large skillet, heat the oil on medium-high heat. Add onion and saute; add bell pepper and garlic and continue to saute about 5 minutes. Add ground meat and stir. Add seasonings, capers and olives and continue to cook until meat is browned and liquid is absorbed, but mixture is not dry.

Remove center seed from chayote and discard. Remove some of the center flesh. If you wish, mash and add to ground meat mixture, or discard. Place chayotes in a greased glass baking dish. (If you use tomato sauce, don't grease the dish, put sauce in the bottom of the dish instead.) Fill the hollows with ground meat mixture. Sprinkle bread crumbs on top and dot with butter or drizzle with oil. Bake at 400 degrees (F.) until top is browned, about 20 minutes.

Serves 4.

Crepas de Chaya
Chaya Crepes

These crepes have chaya in the sauce as well as the filling. The recipe comes from a government publication on the virtues of chaya put out by the State of Quintana Roo on the peninsula's Caribbean coast..

Crepe batter:
2 oz. (55 grams) melted butter
6 eggs
¾ cup sifted flour
½ cup milk
¼ cup beer
Salt

Filling:
1½ lbs. chaya leaves, about 3 bunches (use spinach or Swiss chard)
4 Tbls. olive oil
1 white onion, minced
1 clove garlic, minced
2 Tbls. soy sauce
¼ cup sour cream or Mexican crema
Salt and pepper to taste

Sauce:
4 Tbls. butter
2 Tbls. flour
2 cups milk
1 cup chaya, steamed
Salt and pepper to taste
Grated cheese (Manchego, Gruyere or Swiss) for topping

>>>>>

Crepes de Chaya continued

For the crepes: Mix all of the ingredients together in a blender and let them rest in the refrigerator for about 30 minutes. Melt some butter in a non-stick skillet and ladle in about 2 tablespoons of batter for each crepe, spreading it thinly and evenly. (Unless you are experienced, it is better to make them one at a time.) Let it cook for about 30 seconds, just until it sets. Flip and heat the other side for about 10 seconds and remove to a large plate.

For the filling: Steam one bunch of chaya and set it aside. Wash remaining chaya; chop in thin strips, chiffonade style. Heat oil in a medium skillet on medium-high heat and saute the onion and garlic for a minute. Add the chopped chaya and continue to saute until it is limp. Add soy sauce, crema, salt and pepper to taste and remove from heat.

For the sauce: Melt butter in a non-stick pan on medium heat and stir in flour gradually. Add the milk and continue stirring. Chop steamed chaya and add along with salt and pepper, stirring to incorporate. When sauce thickens, remove from heat.

Assembly: Put 2 tablespoons chaya mixture down the center of each crepe, roll up and place it in a large baking dish. Pour the white sauce over the top and sprinkle with grated cheese. Bake in a 350-degree (F) oven for about 10 minutes until top is golden.

Serves 6 or 8.

Niños Envueltos
Stuffed Chaya Leaves

The next time you make a picadillo, prepare an extra batch (it freezes well) to use in this dish. Add cooked rice to the picadillo and you have the filling, ready to roll into blanched chaya leaves. You can easily substitute Swiss chard for chaya. (See vegetarian version.)

1 Tbl. oil
1 lb. ground beef and pork mixed
½ onion, minced
2 tomatoes, chopped
2 large cloves garlic, minced
¼ lb. boiled ham, ground
2 stems fresh mint or basil, or substitute 1 tsp. dried
¼ tsp. each cinnamon, cumin, clove
1 Tbl. each chopped capers, raisins, olives, almonds
Salt to taste
40 to 50 medium to large chaya leaves, about ½ pound
1 cup cooked rice
1 large egg
1 Tbl. flour
Salsa de Tomate

Heat oil in a non-stick skillet on medium high and saute the beef and pork. Add onion, tomatoes and garlic, stir and continue to saute. Add ham, mint or basil, cinnamon, cumin, clove along with the capers, raisins, olives and almonds. Continue cooking and stirring until meat is no longer pink. Add salt to taste.

Wash and blanch the chaya leaves in boiling water on medium-high heat. Be careful not to overcook or they will fall apart. Drain and spread out on a clean counter top to dry. Mix rice, egg, flour and picadillo together for the filling. Place a spoonful of filling at the base of a large leaf. Remove the stem and start to roll up, folding the sides over with each turn. If the leaf is too small or thin, use two leaves, or make a patch with a pieces of smaller leaf. Prepare the tomato sauce and simmer the "ninos" in the sauce for 10 to 15 minutes, until well heated. Arrange the roll-ups in a star pattern on a dinner place on top of a pool of tomato sauce.

Yield: 30 or more, enough for 6 entrees

Niños Envueltos Vegetarianos
Vegetarian Stuffed Chaya Leaves

You don't have to be vegetarian to enjoy this tasty appetizer. Once we made them with fresh mint, dry dill, golden raisins and pine nuts, and people wanted to know where we had found grape leaves in Merida.

40 to 50 medium to large chaya leaves, about ½ pound
2 cups cooked rice (1 cup uncooked)
1 large egg
1 Tbl. flour
½ tsp. toasted and crushed oregano
½ cup chopped raisins
¼ cup EACH olives and capers, chopped
½ cup toasted almonds, chopped
Peel from 1 tomato

Wash and quickly blanch the chaya leaves in boiling water. Don't overcook or they will be difficult to handle. Drain and spread leaves out on a clean counter top to dry. Prepare the rice according to directions for Arroz Blanco. Mix cooked rice, egg, flour, raisins, olives, capers and almonds together for the filling. Place a spoonful of filling at the base of a large leaf. Remove the stem and start to roll up, folding the sides over with each turn. If the leaf is too small or thin, use two leaves or make a patch with a pieces of smaller leaf. Carefully place the roll-ups in a vegetable steamer basket and steam over an inch of water for 10 to 15 minutes, until well heated. Cool roll-ups and arrange on a platter decorated with a tomato rose. Serve at room temperature.

Yield: 30 or more.

Pastel de Queso con Chaya
Cheesecake With Chaya

After serving this savory cheesecake at an International Women's Club coffee, I was coaxed into including it in my cookbook, even though it is not authentically Yucatecan. Feel free to substitute spinach or Swiss chard for the chaya.

10 to 12 oz. (about two bags) chaya
1¼ cups Parmesan cheese
½ cup breadcrumbs
3 Tbls. butter, melted
2 lbs. cream cheese, softened
4 large eggs
½ cup finely chopped cebollina (chives)
1 tsp. freshly grated nutmeg
½ tsp. salt
1 tsp. white pepper
1 cup sour cream (or media crema mixed with 1 Tbl. Vinegar)

Wash and steam the chaya in a little water for about 5 minutes. Drain well and squeeze out as much water as possible; chop and set aside. Spray a 9-inch springform pan with non-stick cooking spray and preheat the oven to 350 (F.) degrees. Put ¼ cup of the Parmesan cheese and all of the breadcrumbs in the pan. Add the melted butter; mix well and press evenly into the bottom of the pan.

In a large bowl, beat the cream cheese until smooth, adding the eggs one at a time. Add the remaining 1 cup Parmesan cheese, cebollina, nutmeg, salt and pepper and continue beating. Fold in the sour cream and chopped chaya by hand and blend well. Pour the mixture into the prepared pan and bake on the center rack of the oven for 45 minutes. Turn off the oven and leave the door ajar for 30 minutes. Remove and continue to cool on a rack for 15 minutes. To store, place in refrigerator with plastic wrap directly on top of the cake for up to 2 days. Remove outer ring and place on a serving platter. Serve as an appetizer, at room temperature, spread on plain crackers

Serves 15 to 20.

Tortitas de Chaya
Chaya Patties

There are many variations of chaya patties. One uses eggs and a little wheat flour instead of corn masa to make a light, lacy patty. This one, with corn masa, is the most traditional. Also known as Gorditas de Chaya, sometimes they are stuffed with a picadillo or cheese. You can also make little balls or Bolitas de Chaya with this recipe, in which case you might want to add a little grated cheese to the mixture and serve them as an appetizer.

15 large or 30 small chaya leaves
½ onion, chopped
1 habanero chile, if desired
2 cups masa harina or 1 lb. prepared masa
¼ cup flour
½ to 1 cup chaya cooking water
2 tsps. salt
¼ tsp. freshly grated nutmeg
2 Tbls. liquid lard or oil

Clean and chop the chaya leaves, removing the stems. In a medium-sized saucepan heat about ½ cup water on medium-high heat. Add the chaya, chopped onion and whole habanero, cover and steam about 10 minutes. Drain, reserving water. Mix reserved cooking water, and additional fresh water as needed, with masa to form a dough. Add salt and nutmeg, steamed chaya and onion and mix. Let the dough rest a bit and then form into tiny, thin patties and fry in lard or oil on medium-high heat until golden brown on both sides. Serve with fresh tomato sauce.

Makes 30 to 40, depending on size of patties.

Soups, Salads and Eggs

Soups can be as simple as a chicken broth with diced vegetables and rice, as hearty as lentil stew, or as delicate as the region's famous Sopa de Lima made with an especially aromatic type of lime.

Salad is often no more than a garnish of lettuce, tomato and onion dressed with salt and pepper and a bit of fresh lime or sour orange juice. Or it may be a garnish of pickled vegetables. When lettuce, spinach or cabbage are used in a salad, they are often prepared chiffonard style, with the greens thinly sliced into short strips. Additional raw vegetables such as carrots, jicama, tomato, cucumber and avocado are sliced or chopped and artfully arranged on top of the chiffonard. Mayonnaise-bound salads are also found in the region, obvious imports from the north.

Eggs – fried, scrambled and poached – are eaten for breakfast or supper, accompanied by beans, *pan frances* or tortillas and some kind of salsa. Huevos Motuleños, a regional specialty, are in a class by themselves — a breakfast or brunch entree fit for royalty. Hard-cooked eggs figure prominently in some traditional Mayan dishes as well, such as Papadzules.

Sopa de Lima

Chicken Soup with Lime and Tortilla Strips

This signature dish from the Yucatan has many versions, but we always come back to this one. If you have chicken broth on hand, start with it instead of water. The indigenous lima, with a navel-like bump on its blossom end, should not be confused with the limon (lime). Sweetly aromatic, it is mild in flavor. Outside the Yucatan, the best substitute is a Myers lemon.

10 cups water
1 tsp. oregano, toasted and crumbled
2 garlic cloves
1 medium onion, quartered
1 tsp. EACH salt and freshly ground pepper
2 whole large chicken breasts
3 limas (or Myers lemons), sliced in thin rounds
6 corn tortillas cut in strips, fried and drained on paper towels
1 Tbl. oil
1 medium white onion, finely chopped
2 medium tomatoes, finely chopped
1 green bell pepper, finely chopped
Salt and pepper to taste

Bring water to boil in a large pot on high heat along with oregano, garlic, quartered onion, salt and pepper to taste. Rinse chicken, add to pot; return to the boil and simmer on medium heat for about 20 minutes. Remove chicken and set aside while the broth continues to simmer, uncovered on medium-low heat. When cool enough to handle, shred or cut the chicken into bite-sized pieces.

Heat oil in a skillet on medium-high heat and saute the chopped onion until it is translucent; add tomato and bell pepper and continue sauteing a few minutes. Don't overcook. Add salt and pepper to taste.

Assembly: Strain the broth; return it to the stove and add the sauteed vegetables along with half of the sliced limes; let this simmer 10 minutes. Add the chicken and the rest of the lime. Serve immediately accompanied by the crispy fried tortilla strips on a separate plate to be added just before eating in order to ensure their crisp texture.

Serves 8.

Sopa de Ajo
Garlic Soup

This soup is reputed to have restorative powers for those who suffer the aftereffects of too much of the night before. Garlic is also said to be a great weapon against the common cold and flu.

1 head garlic
Oil or lard
3 tomatoes, seeded and finely chopped
1 white onion, peeled and finely chopped
1 green Bell pepper, seeded and finely chopped
4 cups chicken broth
Salt
1 small French roll or bolillo
4 eggs

Peel and mash the garlic while the oil or lard is heating on medium-high heat in a sturdy skillet. Add the garlic to the hot oil and brown quickly. Remove the browned garlic and add the tomatoes, onion and green pepper and saute until the onion is golden. In a Dutch oven or deep skillet, heat the broth on medium-high heat and add salt to taste, the browned garlic and the fritanga of sauteed vegetables. Bring it to a boil, lower the heat and simmer a few minutes. Meanwhile, slice the bread and toast or fry it in the same pan you used for the vegetables. When you are ready to serve, pour the simmering broth in four soup bowls and crack a fresh egg into each. Cut the toasted bread into little squares and add some to each bowl.

Serves 4.

Sopa de Bolitas de Masa Con Chaya
Masa Ball Soup With Chaya

The English translation of this delicious soup sounds strikingly like one of Jewish origin. However, the balls or dumplings are corn masa, not matza, and they are mixed with chaya. This is peasant food at its finest. Start with a good broth and you will have a fine soup.

½ lb. chaya (spinach or Swiss chard)
½ lb. fresh corn masa
2 tsps. salt
1 Tbl. flour
1 tomato
¼ bell pepper
¼ large white onion
1 tsp. oil
1 qt. chicken, turkey or beef broth
Cilantro leaves and limes for garnish

Wearing rubber gloves to avoid a rash, rinse and stem the chaya. In a deep pot, cook the chaya in about 1 quart of salted boiling water for about 5 minutes. Remove and drain the chaya, reserving the cooking water. In a medium bowl, mix masa with salt and flour; add just enough chaya cooking water to make it pliable. Chop the chaya in tiny pieces. Blend it into the masa and roll into 1-inch balls. In a large non-stick skillet, heat ¼ inch oil on high heat until almost smoking and brown the bolitas until golden. Don't crowd them, let them float as they cook. Drain on paper towels.

Meanwhile, seed and chop the tomato. Chop the bell pepper and onion. In a large stew pot or Dutch oven, heat the oil over medium heat. Add the tomato, green pepper and onion and saute until tender. Add chicken broth to this fritanga and bring it to a boil on medium-high heat. Add the bolitas and return to a boil. Lower heat and simmer a few minutes. Serve with chopped cilantro leaves and a lime wedge. A glass of French Rhone or a white Bordeaux and crusty French bread are nice accompaniments.

Serves 4.

Potaje de Lenteja
Lentil Stew

Mediterranean or Spanish influence is evident in this hearty version of Lentil Stew, enriched with pork, chorizo, bacon and/or ham.

1 lb. lentils
1 large garlic clove
¼ tsp cumin
1 stalk epazote, if desired
6 slices bacon, chopped
¼ lb. EACH ham and chorizo, chopped
¼ EACH bell pepper, white onion, chopped
1 medium tomato, chopped
½ inch piece Achiote dissolved in ¼ cup water from lentil pot
1 lb. pork leg or loin
Salt to taste
2 carrots, peeled, quartered
1 EACH pattypan squash, chayote, peeled, seeded, cubed
1 EACH potato, plantain, sour orange
½ bunch cilantro

Rinse lentils and put them in a large pot with 3 quarts water; bring to boil on high heat; add garlic, cumin and epazote and lower heat to simmer.

In a medium-size pan, fry bacon, chorizo and ham for about 10 minutes over medium heat; add pepper and onion and continue sauteing five minutes. Add tomato and dissolved achiote. Simmer about 10 minutes and set aside.

When lentils begin to soften, cut pork into large chunks and add to lentils, along with salt and cook about 30 minutes. Add carrots, pattypan and chayote squash to lentils. Peel and dice potato; peel plantain and cut into large chunks and add both to soup. Simmer 15 minutes. Add the fritanga of sauteed meat and vegetables and simmer 15 minutes more. Serve with chopped cilantro on top, a squeeze of sour orange, and bolillos or French bread.

Serves 6.

Potaje de Frijol Blanco
White Bean Stew

This hearty dish of Mediterranean ancestry is just as tasty with red beans.

½ lb. small white beans soaked overnight
1 stem of epazote, if available
2 tsp. salt
1 lb. pork loin or leg, cut in 1½-inch chunks
2 small pattypan squash, peeled, seeded
1 medium chayote, peeled, seeded
½ cup finely chopped cabbage
4 oz. smoked ham cut up
1 Tbl. oil
1 large clove garlic
¼ EACH medium bell pepper, white onion
1 tomato
1 lean chorizo sausage, about 4 oz.
2 medium potatoes
1 lime, cut in wedges
½ cup chopped cilantro leaves
Chile Tamulado (habanero chile), if desired

Rinse and drain the pre-soaked beans, cover with water and add epazote. Bring to a boil on high heat and add salt. When beans begin to soften, 30 to 40 minutes depending on age, add the pork. Cut squash and chayote, into 1-inch cubes and add to pot along with cabbage and ham and let it simmer on low heat. Heat oil in a non-stick skillet over medium heat. Mash the garlic and add to the skillet. Finely chop the pepper, onion and tomato and add to the sauteing garlic. Cut the chorizo into 1-inch rounds, remove the skin and add to the skillet. Continue to saute for about 5 minutes. Add this sauteed mixture to the stew and stir to incorporate. Peel and dice the potatoes and add to the stew. Continue cooking about 15 minutes, until beans and vegetables are tender. Serve garnished with cilantro, and lemon wedges and chile sauce on the side.

Serves 8.

Mondongo a la Andaluza
Andalucia Style Tripe Stew

Here in the Yucatan, tripe stew is known as Mondongo. There are two versions: This one is from Spain. Mondongo Kabik is of Mayan influence. Menudo lovers will enjoy this soup for a change of pace.

1 lb. tripe, cleaned
Salt to taste
½ tsp. oregano, toasted and crushed
1 head garlic, roasted
4 potatoes, quartered
½ cup garbanzos pre-soaked
2 ancho chiles
5 Roma tomatoes, chopped
2 tsps. olive oil
1 EACH, white onions, bell pepper, chopped
1 bunch parsley, stemmed and chopped
2 large cloves garlic, chopped
1 small bunch cebollina (chives), chopped
¼ lb. ham, cut up
2 chorizos, 3- to 4-inches each
¼ tsp. EACH black pepper, cinnamon, oregano, cumin, clove
Sprig of mint
½ tsp. saffron
2 xcatic or guero chiles

Clean the tripe and put it in a large pot of water to boil on medium-high heat along with the salt, oregano, roasted garlic and garbanzos. Lower the heat and let it simmer at a low boil. In a small saucepan, bring the ancho chiles to boil on medium-high heat in enough water to cover for 1 minute. Remove, cool to the touch, seed and de-vein. Chop the chiles and put in a blender along with the chopped tomatoes and some cooking liquid. Liquify and strain this mixture into the simmering tripe. Heat olive oil in a skillet. Saute onions, bell pepper, parsley and garlic and saute them in the olive oil over medium heat until the onion starts to turn golden. Add to stew along with potatoes, chives, ham, chorizo and seasonings. Add chiles whole. Cover and simmer, stirring every 20 minutes until the tripe is tender, about an hour.

Serves 6

Crema de Cilantro
Cream of Cilantro Soup

This soup is a specialty of Hacienda Teya, just east of Merida. Instead of croutons, try garnishing it with Salsa de Chiltomate and a dab of sour cream or Mexican crema. For a richer, thicker soup, use a cup of Mexican crema in place of 1 cup milk.

3 stalks celery
1 small white onion
1 small green bell pepper, seeded
2 cloves garlic
2 small carrots
1 medium leek
½ stick butter
3 Tbls. flour
6 cups milk, divided
3-4 bunches cilantro, washed and dried
3 bay leaves
2 tsps. chicken bouillon
1 tsp. cumin
Salt and pepper to taste
Seasoned croutons
4 sprigs cilantro

Wash and roughly chop the celery, onion, bell pepper, garlic, carrots and leek. Melt the butter in a large skillet over medium heat. Saute the vegetables in butter until soft, about 10 minutes. In a blender or food processor, puree the sauteed vegetables along with 2 cups milk and return to pot. Dissolve flour in 2 cups milk and add to pot. Stir until thickened over medium heat. Set aside 4 sprigs of cilantro and put the rest, including stems, in a blender with remaining milk and blend until smooth. Add to pot along with bay leaves, bouillon and cumin. When soup begins to boil, lower heat and simmer a few minutes. Add salt and pepper to taste. Strain soup into bowls and garnish with croutons and cilantro.

Serves 6 to 8.

Cebolla Encurtida
Pickled Red Onions

This salad or relish is most often served with fried fish, roasted chicken, Cochinita Pibil, Panuchos, Poc Chuc, Salbutes, and many other dishes. Crunchy and tangy, it goes well with barbecued meats.

3 red onions, chopped or thinly sliced
1 tsp. oregano
Juice of 2 sour oranges or ¼ cup mild, fruity vinegar
¼ tsp. salt

Marinate the onions in the juice or vinegar along with oregano and salt for at least 1 hour before serving. If you use sour orange, it will keep 2 to 3 days at the most; with vinegar, up to 2 weeks.

Makes about 2 cups.

Betabel En Escabeche
Pickled Beet Salad

Deli counters in most supermarkets offer this deep burgundy-colored dish highlighted by rings of white onion and fresh green cilantro.

3 medium red beets
1 large white onion, sliced in rounds.
1 cup juice of freshly squeezed sour orange, or mild fruity vinegar
½ cup sherry
1 Tbl. vegetable oil
1 tsp. whole black peppercorns
1 tsp. whole allspice
1 tsp. crushed oregano
½ tsp. cumin
1 or 2 roasted habanero chiles, optional
1 bunch cilantro

Wash, trim and steam beets in a covered vegetable steamer with about an inch of water for 30 to 60 minutes on medium-high heat, depending on age and tenderness of beets. Test for tenderness by gently squeezing. Do not pierce or they will lose vitamins as well as color. When tender, remove and cool to the touch; peel and slice into thin rounds. If large, slice rounds in half. Place in a large bowl or glass dish along with most of the sliced onions; reserve large outer rings for garnish. Add sour orange, or vinegar, sherry and oil, along with peppercorns, allspice, oregano and cumin. Stir to blend. Add water if necessary to cover the beets and onions. Add a few whole, roasted habanero chiles, if desired, for added flavor. Stir a few times while it rests several hours before serving. Sprinkle with finely chopped cilantro and large onion rings just before serving.

Serves 6

Ensalada Xec

Jicama and Orange Salad

This salad (pronounced SHECK) is a natural outgrowth of the orchards and back-yard gardens of the rural Maya. Jicama, mandarina (tangerine) and cilantro are the base. Add carrot and avocado for variety and color, if desired.

1 medium jicama
2 to 3 navel oranges or tangerines, seeded
1 small carrot, if desired
½ cup cilantro leaves
1 carrot or avocado, if desired
1 lime or sour orange
Red chile powder

Peel and slice the jicama into thin pieces or matchsticks. Peel and slice the oranges in rounds, removing as much pith as possible. Cut the mandarin in half and section as you would for grapefruit, removing seeds. Peel the carrot and shed into tiny bits, if using. Peel and cut avocado into thin slices or small chunks, if desired. Gently mix the jicama, orange and avocado, if using. Squeeze some lime or sour orange juice on top. Garnish with cilantro leaves, shredded carrot and a sprinkling of chile powder.

Serves 4

Huevos Motuleños
Eggs Motul Style

According to popular belief, this dish was developed in 1921 for visiting dignitaries by the chef of then-Gov. Felipe Carrillo Puerto. The chef was a native of Motul, thus the name Motuleños. Some speculate that Carrillo Puerto's special friend, American journalist Alma Reed, was among the dignitaries for whom this dish was created. After all, he commissioned the lovely song, "Peregrina" for her, so why not a special dish? A favorite in Merida restaurants and hotels, this regional dish makes an impressive brunch entree, as well as a good conversation piece for those unfamiliar with the story of its origin.

16 tortillas, crisped in oil
2 cups refried black beans, heated
8 slices ham, cut in strips
1½ cups cooked peas
16 eggs cooked sunny-side up
Salsa de Tomate
½ lb. Queso fresco or a soft crumbly cheese of your choice
1½ plantains cut in 16 diagonal slices and fried in butter

(It is best to have a helper for this dish, one to fry the eggs, the other to prepare the plates.) Have everything – tortillas, beans, ham, peas, sauce, cheese and plantains – ready before you fry the eggs so they will be hot when you serve them. Place 8 crisp tortillas on 8 plates and spread them with refried beans. Top each with a sunny-side up fried egg. Pour some tomato sauce over each and sprinkle with some cheese. Make a second layer, adding the remaining tortillas, eggs, and the rest of the sauce, equally divided; put ham strips and peas on top of the egg. Add remaining cheese and adorn each plate with 2 slices fried plantain.

Serves 8.

Papadzules

Egg Filled Tortillas in Pumpkin Seed Sauce

In Maya, the word "Papadzul" means food for the lords. This special occasion pre-Columbian dish is made with pumpkin-seed sauce. In the Yucatan you can buy the seeds toasted and ground or already formed into a lovely colored green paste. Traditionally the paste was made by hand and some of the green oil that was released in the process was reserved and used as a garnish. If you make the paste in a blender, you can still work it by hand a few minutes to extract some garnishing oil before adding the additional broth to make the sauce.

10 hard-cooked eggs*
24 tortillas
Papadzules Sauce:
12 to 16 oz. green, hulled pumpkin seeds, or papadzule paste
1 stalk epazote, if available
¼ medium white onion
½ head garlic
2 cups salted chicken broth
Tomato Sauce:
4 tomatoes, seeded and chopped
1 habanero chile, whole
1 onion, chopped
1 tsp. oil
Salt and pepper to taste

Peel and chop the eggs and set aside, along with the tortillas.

For the Papadzules Sauce: Slowly toast pumpkin seeds in a dry skillet on low heat or on a baking sheet in a 300-degree oven for about 20 minutes. Be careful not to brown the pumpkin seeds when toasting, because it will detract from the light green color of the sauce. Meanwhile, in a saucepan, bring chicken broth, epazote, onion and garlic to boil on medium-high heat. In a blender or food processor, grind the toasted seeds. Add ¼ cup strained broth to ground seeds and process to form a paste. (At this point, take the

Papadzules continued

paste out and work it by hand to extract the oil, if you wish.) Gradually add the rest of the broth to make a creamy sauce. Set aside while you prepare the tomato sauce.

For the tomato sauce: In a blender, liquify the chopped and seeded tomatoes. Heat the oil, in a non-stick skillet on medium-high heat and saute the onion. Add the liquified tomato mixture, the whole chile and salt and pepper to taste. Let it simmer until the flavors blend and the sauce thickens, 10 to 15 minutes.

Assembly: In a non-stick frying pan, heat the pumpkin-seed sauce over very low heat until it thickens to a creamy texture. Heat the tortillas on a comal or griddle and dip them in the sauce. Fill each with equal portions of chopped eggs (reserving some chopped egg whites and yolks for garnish) and roll them up. Pour the tomato sauce over the filled tortillas and sprinkle chopped egg on top, alternating rows of whites and yolks. Drizzle with pumpkin seed oil if available.

Serves 8.

*For a heartier main dish, add some cooked and seasoned ground pork to the egg filling.

Crepas Yucatecas
Yucatan-Style Crepes

At one time, Dante's Cafe on the Paseo Montejo in Merida served this updated version of Papadzules, which uses crepes instead of tortillas.

10 hard-cooked eggs
Papadzules Sauce
Tomato Sauce
½ cup unsifted flour
¼ tsp. salt
¾ cup milk
2 eggs
2 Tbls. plus 2 tsps. olive oil
¼ cup chopped cilantro leaves

Prepare hard-cooked eggs, pumpkin-seed sauce and tomato sauce as directed in previous recipe for Papadzules. Keep both sauces warm while you prepare the crepes.

For the crepes: In a small bowl, mix the flour and salt. In a separate bowl, combine milk, eggs and 2 tablespoons olive oil. Add this mixture gradually to the flour and salt, using a whisk to incorporate them. Whisk until smooth. Refrigerate the batter, covered, for 30 minutes. Strain to remove any lumps before using. Heat part of the remaining oil in a small, heavy non-stick skillet on medium-high heat. Using a small ladle or large spoon, pour 2 tablespoons of batter into the pan and spread it evenly and quickly. Cook until lightly browned, about 30 seconds on the first side, flip for 10 more seconds; slide onto a plate and continue with the next crepe. Add more oil as needed to keep crepes from sticking. Make 12 crepes.

Assembly: Put 3 crepes on each of four plates. Put a spoonful of toasted pumpkin seed sauce down the center and fill each crepe with equal portions of chopped eggs, reserving some of the chopped egg for a garnish. Roll them up and top with tomato sauce. Garnish with chopped egg and cilantro.

Serves 4.

Desserts & Beverages

While dessert is likely to be just a piece of fresh fruit, a fine array of cakes and pastries are also found in the Yucatan. A regional standout is Torta de Cielo, a classic European torte made with ground almonds. In contrast to the elegant Torta is the homsepun but equally delicious Pastel de Aviones, a type of refrigerator cake made with cookies and pudding. Perhaps the best know regional dessert is Dulce de Papaya, chunks of papaya cooked in sugar syrup.

Beverages also tend toward the natural, most being made from fresh fruits and grains, like rice and barley. Among "adult" beverages, we need look no further than Campeche, the peninsula's famous walled city, for the origin of the "cocktail."

According to legend, cantina owners in Campeche used to stir mixed drinks with the branch of a colorful plant called "cola de gallo" or cock's tail. Eventually these mixed drinks came to be called cocktails by the foreign sailors and pirates (many of them from England) who frequented the port-side pubs. One of the famous "cocktails" from Campeche is the "Campechana," a variation on the Cuba Libre, made with rum, mineral water and Coke.

Refresco de Cafe

Sweetened Iced Coffee With Ice Cream

This cool, sweet drink, adapted from an old regional cookbook, has European roots. It is nice for a late afternoon drink with friends, a "merienda", or with a good book. Serve with a few cookies or a little piece of Torta de Cielo for a real treat.

1 quart coffee
1 cup cream
¼ cup sugar
1 cup vanilla, chocolate or coffee ice cream

Cool the coffee and add the cream, sugar and HALF of the ice cream. Mix well to incorporate the cream and ice cream. Pour into 8 glasses with chopped ice and top each with a dollop of ice cream.

Serves 8.

Chelada
Cold Beer with Lime Juice and Salt

Here is a very refreshing, very tropical way to drink beer without getting a headache, or so the locals say. Cheladas are popular year round, but especially in the hottest months, May and June. It was during those months that we learned to make them from two grey-haired grandmotherly ladies who were visiting our condo complex on the Gulf. Every afternoon after a swim, they would sit on the patio and drink Cheladas. Be sure to use fresh juice.

Salt
1½ to 2 oz. fresh Mexican lime or lemon juice
5 oz. beer
Ice

Wet the rim of a tall glass with lime juice and dip it in salt, as you would for a margarita. Squeeze fresh lime juice into the glass. Add beer, ice and stir.

Makes 1.

Michelada
Chile Seasoned Beer With Lime

Michelada takes the Chelada a step further, with a few drops of habanero salsa, or Worcestershire (Salsa Inglesa). You can also dip the rim of the glass in chile powder for a lip-tingling treat.

Salt or chile powder
1½ to 2 oz. fresh Mexican lime or lemon juice
5 oz. beer
2 to three drops of habanero or Worcestershire sauce
Ice

Wet the rim of a tall glass with lime juice and dip it in salt or chile powder. Squeeze fresh lime juice into the glass. Add beer, salsa, ice and stir.

Makes 1.

Limonada Aromatica
Aromatic Lemonade

This version of lemonade is adapted from an old regional cookbook. The spices are a lovely addition to the sugar syrup.

1 cup water
1 cup sugar
½ tsp. whole cloves
1 1-inch piece cinnamon stick
4 Mexican limes or lemons

Make a seasoned sugar syrup by bringing the water, sugar, clove and cinnamon stick to a boil over medium high heat in a heavy sauce pan. Remove the peel (not the pith) of one lime or lemon and add it to the sugar syrup and continue cooking over medium heat until it thickens. Remove from heat and add the juice of the 4 limes or lemons; mix well. Use 2 tablespoons of this syrup for each glass of lemonade. Add regular or carbonated water, ice, cubed or chopped.

Serves 6.

Naranjada
Orangeade

Naranjada is the same as limonada but with oranges in place of limes. It is delightfully refreshing. You can make it with sour oranges as well, adjusting the tartness by the amount of sugar you add.

4 sweet or sour oranges
1½ quarts water
Sugar to taste

Squeeze the oranges and strain the juice into a pitcher with 1½ quarts water. Add 2 teaspoons sugar or more to taste. Add ice cubes, stir and serve.

Serves 6

Agua de Cebada
Barley Water

Imagine a soft drink made from barley! That's what cebada is and lots of Yucatecans were raised on it. Although it is difficult to find, you can still buy bottles of cebada soda made by Crystal in the Yucatan. It tastes somewhat like cream soda. Agua de Cebada is a healthier version that you can make at home. If you want to approximate the bottled refresco, use mineral or carbonated water and a few drops of vanilla.

½ cup pearl barley
2-inch piece of cinnamon stick
2 qts. water*
1 cup sugar
Sliced lime

Soak the barley in enough water to cover overnight, or for at least 2 hours. Bring one quart water to boil over high heat and add the drained, soaked barley. Return to boil, cover and lower heat to simmer. Add remaining quart of water and the sugar. Continue to simmer on low heat, covered, for at least one hour. Test the barley to see if it is tender and taste the liquid for sweetness. Add more sugar if desired. Cool and strain into a glass pitcher. Serve in tall glasses with ice and a slice of lime. It is very refreshing. (*If you want to use carbonated water, simmer the barley in 1 quart of water and when it cools, add a quart of soda water and a teaspoon of vanilla.)

Serves 8 to 10.

Campechana
Rum With Coke and Club Soda

Most people are familiar with the refreshing Cuba Libre, rum and Coke with fresh lime. This variation comes from the port city of Campeche, alleged home of the cocktail or "cola de gallo," as they say in Spanish. If you like rum, but prefer a drink that is not too sweet, you will enjoy the Campechana.

3 ice cubes
1 jigger rum
3 oz. cola
3 oz. club soda or mineral water
Lime slice

Put ice cubes in a tall glass. Pour in a jigger (1½ oz.) of rum, then fill half the glass with cola and finish off with club soda. Cut the edge of the lime slice and slip it onto the rim of the glass.

Makes 1 cocktail.

Horchata

Rice, Almond and Cinnamon Drink

Horchata is like liquid rice pudding. Although found in other parts of Mexico, horchata is most at home in this hot, tropical region. It is also made without the almonds.

1 cup rice
¼ cup almonds, without skins
2 tsps. ground cinnamon
½ cup sugar or more to taste

Soak the rice and almonds separately in enough water to cover overnight. In the morning, drain the rice and grind it in a blender or food processor as fine as possible. Strain the almonds as well and blend them to a paste. Mix ground rice and almond paste in a blender or food processor along with cinnamon and about a quart of water and sugar to taste. Serve over ice.

Makes 4 8-oz. servings.

Torta de Cielo
Classic Almond Torte

This elegant cake is the quintessential special occasion dessert. It transports easily, requires no filling or icing yet it makes a nice presentation.

2 cups whole peeled almonds
1 Tbl. flour
1½ cups sugar
6 eggs, separated
1 tsp. cream of tarter
1 tsp. vanilla or almond flavoring
Powdered sugar for sprinkling

Preheat the oven to 325 degrees F. Grease a 9- or 10-inch spring-form cake pan and line with wax paper or parchment, also greased. In a food processor, grind the almonds with a little of the sugar until they are very fine and almost form a paste. Add the flour and process until well mixed.

In a large clean bowl, beat the egg whites with cream of tartar until soft peaks form; add the sugar, little by little; continue beating until the peaks are stiff and shiny. Beat the yolks separately and add them a little at a time, folding them into the beaten whites carefully; fold in the almond and flour mixture with a spatula and dribble in the vanilla.

Pour the mix into the prepared pan and bake for 40 minutes or until the cake is golden. Remove and cool on a wire rack for about 5 minutes. Un-mold and allow to cool completely. Put the cake on a large cake platter lined with a paper doily and sprinkle with powdered sugar.

Serves 8 to 10.

Pastel de Galletas Aviones
Refrigerator Cake

You can substitute regular or cinnamon Graham crackers, lemon or chocolate flavored cookies, but don't be tempted to use prepared pudding for the cream layers in this old-fashioned cake. The Crema de Chocolate and Crema Española are superb.

2 cups strong coffee
½ cup sugar
2 oz. coffee-flavored liqueur, optional
1 box Aviones (Graham or similar square or rectangular cookies)
<u>**Crema de Chocolate:**</u>
½ cup cocoa powder
1½ cups sugar
1 Tbl. cornstarch
¼ tsp. salt
2 tsps. vanilla
2 cups milk
1 Tbl. butter
<u>**Crema Española:**</u>
2 cups milk
½ cup sugar
2 egg yolks
1 Tbl. cornstarch
1 tsp. vanilla
<u>**Merengue Italiano:**</u>
3 eggs whites
1 cup sugar
1 Tbl. water or lemon juice

Make a coffee syrup by heating 2 cups strong coffee with ½ cup sugar and some coffee-flavored liqueur, if you wish. Bring to a boil and continue stirring until sugar dissolves and the mixture thickens. Remove from heat and let it cool while you prepare the pan. Line the bottom and sides of an 8-x-8-inch baking dish with enough plastic wrap that it overlaps the sides.

>>>>

Pastel continued

Chocolate cream filling: In a saucepan, blend the dry ingredients together. Mix in the vanilla and milk. Put the pan over medium low heat and cook, stirring constantly until it thickens. Remove from heat and stir in the butter. Set aside to cool.

Crema Española: In a saucepan, mix the milk and sugar. Separate out ½ cup of this sweetened milk and put it in a bowl. Whisk 2 egg yolks and the cornstarch into the bowl. (Reserve egg whites for the meringue.) Bring the rest of the milk to boil over medium heat. Once it is boiling, add the milk-egg-cornstarch mixture and continue stirring constantly so that no lumps form. When thickened, remove from heat, stir in vanilla and keep stirring until cooled slightly.

Assembly: One at a time, dip the cookies in the coffee-flavored syrup and cover the bottom of the dish lined with plastic wrap with one layer of cookies. Spread half of the chocolate filling on top of the cookies. Put another layer of syrup-soaked cookies on top and press down a bit. (If the cookies are rectangular, turn them in the opposite direction from the first layer for stability.) Add the cream filling and another layer of soaked cookies. Finish with the rest of the chocolate filling and a final layer of cookies. Put the cake in the freezer for about 30 minutes while you prepare the meringue topping. Carefully remove the cake from the dish using the plastic wrap to hold it and put it on a serving platter. Remove plastic wrap and spread the meringue over the top and sides. Return to refrigerator until ready to serve.

Meringue topping: Beat the egg whites until soft peaks form. Heat the sugar and water or lemon juice over medium heat to form a sugar syrup. Do not brown the sugar. When it reaches a soft ball stage, slowly add it to the meringue while beating continuously to form a meringue frosting.

Serves 6 to 8.

Dulce de Papaya
Papaya Cooked in Syrup

This thoroughly regional dessert is prepared and served in the humblest homes and the best regional restaurants.

1 medium papaya, not too ripe
1 qt. water
2 cups sugar
1 small cinnamon stick
1 tsp. vanilla

Peel and seed papaya and cut into large chunks. Bring water and sugar to boil over high heat. Add papaya, cinnamon, broken into pieces, and vanilla. Lower heat and simmer uncovered for about 2 hours until the papaya has absorbed most of the syrup and takes on a spongy texture. Serve with a mild cheese and crackers.

Serves 8.

Sorbete de Limon
Lime Sherbet

From the extensive, hand-written recipe collection of Bertha Baeza de Rosado, a native Meridana and the mother of a good friend, comes this cooling dessert.

1½ cups sugar
4 cups milk*
Zest of 1 lime
Juice of 2 limes
1 egg white, beaten

Put the sugar and milk in a saucepan over medium heat and cook, stirring occasionally, until all of the sugar dissolves, 10 to 15 minutes. Let it cool and pour into ice cube trays to freeze. When it is partially hardened, remove and dump into a bowl. Add the grated lime zest and juice and the beaten egg white and stir to blend well. Return to the freezer in a bowl and freeze. Serve a scoop of sorbete with lemon or lime cookies on the side.

Makes 1 quart.

*For richer flavor, use ½ evaporated and ½ regular milk.

Crema de Coco
Fresh Coconut Pudding

This wonderfully rich home-style dessert is found in a few regional restaurants.

2 or 3 fresh coconuts or 3 cups shredded, unsweetened coconut
4 cups milk
1 tsp. vanilla
6 oz. cornstarch
1 12-oz. can sweetened condensed milk
¾ cup sugar
1 2½-inch stick cinnamon
1 tsp. ground cinnamon

Poke a hole in the coconut, drain out the liquid and discard. Break open the coconut by inserting a small screw driver or ice pick in the hole and tapping the end with a hammer until the coco cracks open. Peel the coconut flesh away from the husk and chop the coconut into small pieces. Grind it very fine (A food processor works well for this.) Put a quarter to a third of the ground coconut and an equal portion of milk in a blender and puree for at least 1 minute. Strain the coconut and milk puree, using a fine mesh strainer, into a large pot. Push down on the ground coconut to press out the liquid; repeat with remaining ground coconut and milk.

Heat mixture over medium heat. Add vanilla, cornstarch and condensed milk, stirring constantly. Gradually add sugar, continuing to stir for about 10 minutes. Add cinnamon stick and continue stirring until mixture thickens, about 5 more minutes. Remove cinnamon stick and pour coconut cream into glass goblets. Refrigerate until serving time. Serve sprinkled with ground cinnamon.

Makes 8 servings.

Caballeros Pobres
French Toast With Raisins and Syrup

Invented as a way to use up day-old bread, this dessert is sold in bakeries throughout the Yucatan. Make it with a milk syrup instead of simple sugar syrup, and it takes on the character of bread pudding and the name changes from poor gentlemen to rich gentlemen, "Caballeros Ricos." Add a touch of rum or a fruity liqueur and you have a special occasion dessert.

1 loaf of day-old French bread
2 eggs
½ Tbl. sugar
1 Tbl. milk
Oil or butter
1 cup water or milk
½ cup sugar
½ tsp. cinnamon
¼ cup raisins
Rum or fruit-flavored liqueur, if desired

Slice the bread into rounds and toast. Beat the eggs with the sugar and tablespoon of milk. Heat oil or butter in a large non-stick skillet over medium heat. Dip the toasted bread in the egg mix and fry in oil or butter until golden. Place the bread in an oven-proof pan. In a small saucepan, heat a cup of water or milk over medium heat. Add the sugar and cinnamon and stir to dissolve the sugar. Sprinkle raisins over the bread. When sugar is dissolved, remove from heat, add about ¼ cup rum or liqueur, if desired, and pour over the bread and raisins. Sprinkle a little more cinnamon on top.

Bake about 20 minutes at 350 degrees, or until the syrup begins to boil. (You can also let it simmer in a skillet on top of the stove instead of in the oven.)

Serves 6 to 8.

Pastel de Mango
Mango Crisp

This recipe is from a fund-raising cookbook put out by the International Women's Club of Merida. It is a wonderful adaptation of local ingredients to the all-American Apple Crisp. The addition of an egg helps keep the topping crisp in humid climates.

4 cups slices, peeled mangos
1 cup sifted flour
1 cup sugar
1 tsp. baking powder
¾ tsp. salt
1 tsp. cinnamon
1 tsp. freshly ground nutmeg
1 egg
½ cup melted butter
½ cup chopped pecans (optional)

Line a buttered 8-by-8-by-2-inch baking dish with mango slices. Sift dry ingredients togther and work in egg with pastry blender, or in a food processor, until it reaches the consistency of coarse crumbs. Sprinkle mixture on top of mango slices. Drizzle melted butter on top. Sprinkle with chopped pecans and bake at 375 degrees for 30-35 minutes, or until the top is browned. Serve with whipped cream or vanilla ice cream if you wish.

Serves 6.

Queso Napolitano
Italian-Style Flan

    Flan and Queso Napolitano are practically synonymous. Although it is not of Yucatecan origin, this is one of the region's most popular desserts. Add a teaspoon of grated orange peel for a nice accent. Or add a small package of cream cheese, like my neighbor does, for a really creamy rendition. This recipe is for oven baked flan, but you can also make it quite easily and successfully in a double boiler on top of the stove. Actually the stove-top method is very popular in the Yucatan where it is often too hot to turn on the oven. Stove-top flan takes a little longer, depending on the size of the double-boiler, up to 1 hour.

1½ cups sugar for caramelizing
1 can sweetened condensed milk
1 can evaporated milk
1 tsp. vanilla
5 eggs

    In a small saucepan, slowly melt the sugar with a teaspoon or so of water until it caramelizes, being careful not to burn it. Pour the caramelized sugar syrup into a round Pyrex, about 8 inches across, or in 6 individual cups. Put it in the freezer for a few minutes. Meanwhile, mix the rest of the ingredients in a blender or with a mixer. Don't over-blend. You don't want a lot of foam. Pour the mixture on top of the caramelize sugar. Put the dish inside a larger pan. Pour warm water into the outer pan, filling it halfway; bake for 30 to 40 minutes at 325 degrees F. (I once used a round mold which I placed in an electric wok, partially filled with water, and steam/baked it that way so I wouldn't have to turn on the oven on a hot day.) The flan is ready when a knife inserted in the middle comes out clean, usually about 30 minutes. Cool in a pan of cold water, then un-mold onto a serving plate. Serve slices with an extra dollop of caramelize sugar.

Serves 6 or 8.

Resource Directory

Recados and Salsas

La Perla Spice Company
Santa Ana, CA
800- DEL-MAYAB
FAX: (714) 543-4421
www.delmayab.com   or   www.laperlaspice.com

El Yucateco
P.O. Box 783
Eagle Pass, TX
800-SALSA-42 or (830) 757-0472; FAX (830) 757-2405
www.elyucateco.com

Chaya and Epazote Plants and Seeds

Echo Seed Sales
17430 Durrance Rd.
North Ft. Myers FL 33917

Fairchild Tropical Gardens
Dade County, Florida
(305) 667-1651 Ext. 317 or 325

Taylor's Herb Garden
1535 Lone Oak Road, Vista
CA 92084
(619) 727-3485.

Shepherd's Garden Seeds
30 Irene St.,
Torrington, CT 06790
(860) 482-3638

Bibliography

America's First Cuisines by Sophie D. Coe (University of Texas Press)

The Ancient Maya by Alberto Ruz Lhuillier (Editorial Dante S.A. de C.V.) Merida, Yucatan

Cocina Yucateca Traditional by Silvia Luz Carrillo Lara (Editorial Dante S.A. de C.V.)
        Mexico D.F.

El Libro de Los Guisos de Chaya by Government of Quintana Roo, ed. Jose Diaz-Bolio
        Merida, Yucatan

Ayer y Hoy en la Cocina Yucateca by Maria Luiza Montes de Oca de Castro, (3rd Edition)
        Merida, Yucatan

Cocina Yucateca by Lucrecia Ruz Vda. Baqueiro, (16th Edition) Merida, Yucatan

Entre el Mar y la Milpa, Cocina del Mar by Programa de Apoyo a las Culturas
        Municipales y Comunitarias de Yucatan, Merida, Yucatan

Manual Practico de la Cocina Libanese by Maria Manzur de Borge, (4th Edition) Merida,
        Yucatan

Cocina Yucateca by Nimo Neri (Selector, S.A. de C.V.) Mexico, D.F.

Atlas Cultural de Mexico e Gastronomia by Secretaria de Education Publica, Instituto
        Nacional de Antropologia e Historia (Grupo Editorial Planeta) Mexico, D.F.

Yucatan Cuisine of the Hacienda Teya (Editorial Dante S.A. de C.V.) Merida, Yucatan

Comida Campechana, Guia Gastronomica Mexico Desconocido (Editorial Jilguero S.A.
        de C.V.) Mexico, D.F.

Comida Yucateca, Guia Gastronomica Mexico Desconocido (Editorial Jilguero S.A. de
        C.V.) Mexico, D.F.

Incidents of Travel in Yucatan, John Lloyd Stephens (Dover Publishing)

Recipe Index